DATE DUE

OC 9 98			
OC 31 '98			
NO 19 98			
MR 21 00			
MR 22 01			
AP 16 '01			
MY 7 01			
MY 30 '01			

Did Marco Polo go to China?

By the same author

non-fiction
Chinese Illustration
A Companion to China
Oriental Gardens (with Norah Titley)
The Blue Guide to China

fiction
Stones of the Wall (translator)

Did Marco Polo go to China?

FRANCES WOOD

WestviewPress

A Division of HarperCollins*Publishers*

NOTE ON THE TEXT
I have decided to retain the spelling, punctuation,
errors and oddities of the original register keepers,
journal writers, etc., especially in the transcription
of medieval French and Latin, for which correction
would be inappropriate.

Published in 1996 in the United States of America by Westview Press,
5500 Central Avenue, Boulder, Colorado 80301-2877.

First published in Great Britain in 1995 by Martin Secker & Warburg
Limited, an imprint of Reed Books Limited, Michelin House, 81 Ful-
ham Road, London sw3 6rb and Auckland, Melbourne, Singapore and
Toronto

A CIP catalog record for this book is available from the Library of
Congress.
ISBN 0-8133-8998-4 (cloth)

The paper used in this publication meets the requirements of the American National Standard for Permanence of Paper for Printed Library
Materials z39.48-1984.

10   9   8   7   6   5   4   3   2   1

Contents

Acknowledgements

Thanks first to Peter Hopkirk for being so shocked at the suggestion nearly twenty years ago and for remaining encouragingly appalled for so long. Thanks, too, to Sir Matthew Farrar and Maurice Smith for interest and erudition at the right moments; and to my parents for much extra grandparenting to the delight and improvement of the recipient. As will be clear, I have relied upon the work of scholars of the distant and recent past, notably Colonel Sir Henry Yule, Paul Pelliot, Moule, Latham, Herbert Franke, and Leonardo Olschki. I do hope readers might go back to these venerable sources where, especially in Yule's *Travels* and in anything written by Leonardo Olschki, I think they will find much of interest.

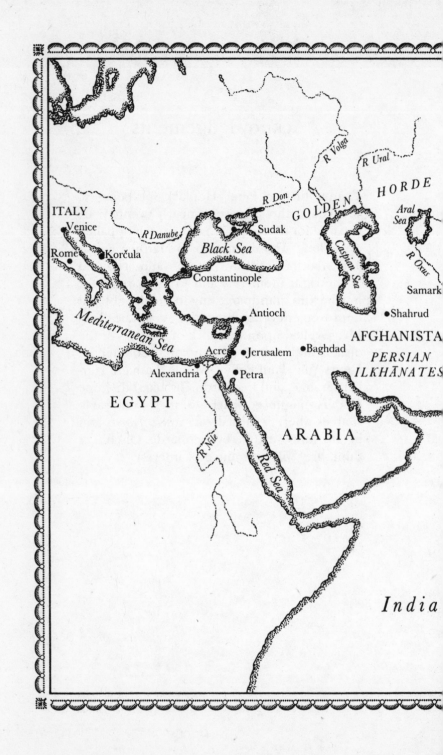

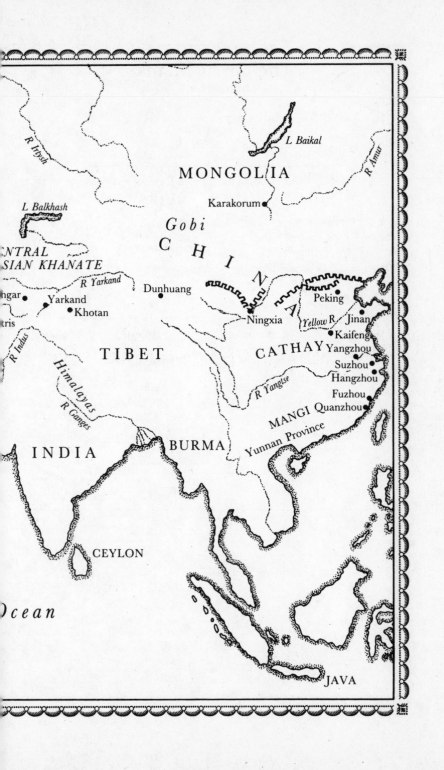

The Great Khans
(numbered)

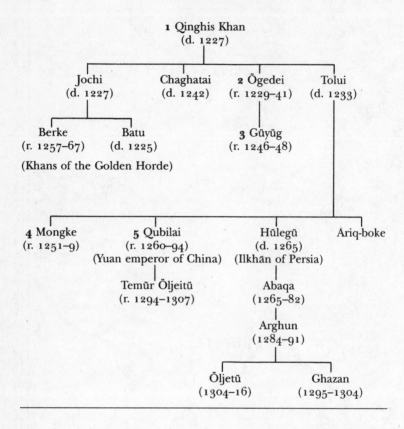

1 Qinghis Khan
(d. 1227)

Jochi
(d. 1227)

Chaghatai
(d. 1242)

2 Ögedei
(r. 1229–41)

Tolui
(d. 1233)

Berke
(r. 1257–67)

Batu
(d. 1225)

3 Güyüg
(r. 1246–48)

(Khans of the Golden Horde)

4 Mongke
(r. 1251–9)

5 Qubilai
(r. 1260–94)
(Yuan emperor of China)

Hülegü
(d. 1265)
(Ilkhān of Persia)

Ariq-boke

Temür Öljeitü
(r. 1294–1307)

Abaqa
(1265–82)

Arghun
(1284–91)

Öljetü
(1304–16)

Ghazan
(1295–1304)

Did Marco Polo go to China?

Introduction

Seven hundred years ago, three men stepped off a small galley onto the stone-paved quayside of Venice. They staggered slightly, their legs unused to firm ground after weeks at sea. There was no one to meet them and their homecoming would have passed quite unnoticed, had their tattered clothing not singled them out. They had 'a certain indescribable smack of the Tartar both in air and accent, having indeed all but forgotten their Venetian tongue'.[1] They wore filthy leather knee-boots and padded silk robes, bound at the waist with more silk, the shaggy fur linings visible through gaping tears in the once fine material. The ragged robes reached only to their knees and were fastened across the chest with round brass buttons, in the Mongol style.

This was how the return of Marco Polo was described, some 200 years after the event. The story-teller, one Giovanni Baptisto Ramusio, went on to tell of how Marco Polo, his uncle and his father, who had all been away for over twenty years, returned to the family home. There, they threw off their ragged robes and put on long Venetian gowns of scarlet silk which reached to the ground. Then, taking their filthy and ragged Mongol robes, they tore at the linings.

Emeralds, rubies, carbuncles, diamonds and sapphires fell to the ground from hiding places in the seams.

Though everyone knows the name Marco Polo, the details of his travels are probably less well-known than those of Christopher Columbus. Most people might associate him with a journey to China and quite a number might identify the story of the return of the ragged traveller. Nevertheless, he ranks in the popular imagination somewhere near the great pioneering voyagers like Columbus, Vasco da Gama and Magellan.

What most people don't seem to know is that a very serious challenge to Marco Polo's popular status has been raised by the most eminent of the German Mongolists.[2] German Mongolists may not, I admit, form a large lobby, but their researches are not to be lightly dismissed, particularly since they represent the most recent and thorough investigation in a long history of academic uncertainty. These serious doubts have not, however, had any effect on Marco Polo's popular position, and the legend is repeated endlessly.

Contemporary children's books, short on text and long on pictures, almost invariably seize on the link between medieval China and Europe that Marco Polo represents. It is as if the vast distances and differences, the mountains, deserts and cultural variations that separate Europe and Peking, are best traversed in shorthand through the person of Marco Polo. It is not only in children's books, either, that he plays a significant role as a cultural missionary. Legend has it that he is responsible for the introduction of noodles to Italy, or spaghetti to China, depending on where you stand, and he has also been credited with the inspiration for Italian ice-cream.

Virtually every book about medieval China, whether popular or scholarly, makes considerable reference to the contents of Marco Polo's book, the *Divisament dou Monde* (*Description of the World*). When I studied Chinese at Cambridge, I dutifully included paragraphs from his description of the city of Peking in my essays, and when I began my Ph.D. thesis on the domestic architecture of Peking, I probably paid more attention to Marco Polo than to many others. My thesis was restricted to the period 1860–1930, but the way Peking's traditional courtyard houses slotted into the regular chessboard pattern of streets still recalled the vanished capital of the Mongol Yuan dynasty (1279–1360) that is described in his book.

Later, I spent a year in Peking between 1975 and 1976 studying at the Languages Institute, a dusty complex in the north-western suburbs, which turned out to have a sort of connection with Marco Polo. The hour-long bicycle ride into town passed by a high, shrub-covered dyke. The ride was a rural one then, with peasants clad in thick padded clothes bending over their crops in misty fields, and tiny, low, grey farmhouses. It was some time before I realised that the dyke was part of the old wall surrounding Yuan-dynasty Peking that had enclosed acres of grazing land for the once-nomadic Mongol rulers. After the recapture of the city by the (Chinese) Ming ruler in 1360, new city walls had been built far to the south, leaving only this remnant running along Xueyuan lu.

When I transferred to the History Department of Peking University, I rarely passed the Mongol wall on my way into town, for the University was further to the north-west, but I still spent most afternoons on my bike, trying to photograph as much as I could of the traditional domestic architecture (a difficult task because of the enclosed nature of the courtyard houses and the enormous suspicion of foreigners at the time). In doing so I became familiar with most of the tiny lanes that lay between the main streets, and all the more conscious of the chessboard layout of the city that Marco Polo first described to Europeans in the late thirteenth century.

It was when I returned to London and my job in the

Chinese section of the Library of the School of Oriental and African Studies that Marco Polo resurfaced. Amongst the students, I was closest to those who, like me, had been students in China during the Cultural Revolution (1966–76). We formed quite a close group, united through our bizarre experiences as 'worker-peasant-soldier' students when we transplanted rice in paddy fields, tied up Chinese cabbage to make it heart and then had to eat nothing else from November to March, and learned how to throw hand grenades at the British Council's expense as part of our compulsory sporting activities on Wednesday afternoons.

Craig Clunas had been in China the year before me and returned to do a Ph.D. at the School of Oriental and African Studies on Mongolian sequels to the *Dream of the Red Chamber.* He told me about the German Mongolists' doubt that Marco Polo had ever reached China and, in a small article on early travellers to China for a *Times* supplement on trade published in 1981, I ended my piece with a casual suggestion that, despite his popular image, Marco Polo should perhaps not be numbered amongst the early visitors to China – and thus provoked much more horror than I could have imagined. The next year, Craig followed with a longer article, again in *The Times*, and we occasionally discussed the possibility of writing a book about it, preferably with the help of a Persian/Arabic medievalist, but we never got round to it.

So here I go, alone.

1

The bare details

Though most people know the name of Marco Polo, very few, if challenged, admit to having actually read his book. Leaving the academic doubts of contemporary scholars and the problems of spaghetti and ice-cream aside for the moment, Marco Polo's own book and the claims made in it are enormously important, for most of what we know (or are told) about Marco Polo is to be found in one or more versions of his own work.

Probably written in 1298, the *Description of the World* begins with a short Prologue which offers the background to the Polo family's travels and describes how the book came to be written. According to the Prologue, Marco Polo's father and uncle, Maffeo and Niccolo Polo, who were Venetian merchants, arrived in Constantinople in 1260 'with their merchandise'.[1] There, they decided 'that they would go across the Black Sea in the hope of a profitable venture . . . and went to Sudak'. At the time, this was one of the main trading posts on the Black Sea, on the northern peninsula, just east of Sevastopol, and it offered access to goods from Russia, Turkey and Persia. 'After staying there for a while, they resolved to go further afield.' They travelled through the territory from the Volga to the Caspian Sea held by the Mongol ruler Berke (ruled 1257–67), and under his authority traded 'very profitably'. However, they found themselves unable to return to Constantinople because war had broken out between Berke and Hülegü, the Mongol ruler of Persia (died 1265). Though Berke and Hülegü were cousins, sharing a grandfather in Qinghis (Chinghiz or Ghenghis) Khan, in 1261–62 they fought the first of a series of wars between the two Khanates based on disputed borders, with both sides claiming North-West Persia and the Caucasus.

The Mongol wars drove the two Polos further eastwards until they found themselves in Karakorum, the home base and capital city of the Mongols, who already controlled much of Central Asia and were beginning to threaten Eastern Europe.

In Karakorum, the two Venetian merchants met the great ruler, or Khan, Qubilai (Kubilai) and, rather than talk of trade, they discussed Christianity with him. Qubilai 'had letters written in the Turkish language to send to the Pope and entrusted them to the two brothers'. 'He sent word to the Pope that he should send up to a hundred men learned in the Christian religion . . . to argue and demonstrate plainly to idolators . . . that their religion is utterly mistaken. . . . Furthermore the Great Khan directed the brothers to bring oil from the lamp that burns above the sepulchre of God in Jerusalem.' He then sent one of his men to accompany the Polos on the first part of their journey and gave him a tablet of gold 'on which it was written that . . . they . . . should be given all the lodging they might need and horses and men'.

They returned to Venice, only to set off again almost immediately in 1271, this time taking Niccolo's son Marco (aged about 17) with them. They had managed to obtain the holy oil, but were not accompanied by any theologians; nor were they able to take a papal letter to Qubilai, since the Church was between popes at the time, but they had been given a covering letter from the papal legate in Acre.

In Karakorum once more, the Polos were welcomed with

'mirth and merrymaking' and Qubilai was much taken with the 'young stripling' Marco. The Khan began to use him as an emissary, sending him off throughout the distant provinces of China, which he was then bringing under Mongol control. (The Mongols had taken north China in 1260 although the south was not fully conquered until 1279.) Marco first went to Yunnan province in south-west China, which took him six months to reach.

It appears that Marco knew how to tell a tale, for the Khan's normal emissaries were scorned by their imperial master as dolts and dunces since they could tell him nothing about the 'customs and usages' of the areas they had visited. Building on their failure, Marco 'paid close attention to all the novelties and curiosities that came his way so that he might retail them to the Great Khan'. On his return to court, he would first deal with the serious business and then 'recount all the remarkable things that he had seen on the way'.

The Prologue is short, only twelve pages long, and it gives an extremely brief overview of the Polos' long stay in China. 'What need to make a long story of it. You may take it for a fact that Messer Marco Polo stayed with the Great Khan fully seventeen years; and in all this time he never ceased to travel on special missions.'

Eventually, the Polos became homesick and begged to be allowed to return home to Italy. They were given permission to depart and returned, not overland as they had come, but mainly by sea, accompanying a young Mongol princess destined to marry the Mongol ruler Arghun, variously described as the Ruler of the Levant or Ilkhān of Persia (who ruled some time after Hülegü, from 1284 to 1291). The trip was a difficult one: only eighteen of the 600 men survived the journey. When this depleted band arrived in Persia, they found that Arghun, too, had died, but they managed to off-load their royal charge on his son, Ghazan. Having discharged their duty, the Polos proceeded on horseback and by sea to Venice, where they arrived, 'in the year of the Incarnation of Christ 1295'. The Prologue concludes, 'Now that I have given you all the substance of the prologue, as you have heard it, I will begin the book . . .'

2

Why go at all?

Why should two Venetian merchants have struggled across the unknown and desolate deserts of Central Asia, let alone retrace their steps bearing holy oil and taking a seventeen-year-old boy with them?

One of the most significant reasons was the growing importance of the trade in exotic products from Asia. The mercantile interest in such rarities that Marco Polo demonstrates throughout his book is hardly surprising given his background as the son and nephew of traders. The economic importance of the Far East and South-East Asia to medieval Europe, which led eventually to the great maritime explorations of Christopher Columbus and Vasco da Gama, lay in the abundance of spices, which both helped in the conservation of food before the days of refrigeration and imparted strong flavours to badly preserved foods.

Marco Polo the merchant mentions the silver mines and fine buckram of Armenia; the crimson silks of Turkey and Tiflis; Georgian oil, which was good for burning (though not eating) and very efficacious against the itch; Baghdadi pearls; cloth of gold from Tabriz; more silks, pistachios, dates and turquoises from Persia; the cheap partridges of the Persian Gulf; rubies, lapis and sesame oil in Central Asia; cotton, flax and hemp from Kashgar; steel and asbestos cloth from Uighuristan; Tangut musk, the best in the world; salt from the mines of Sichuan; ginger and cinnamon, spikenard, galingale and sugar from Bengal; Javanese pepper, nutmeg and cloves; Indian coconuts; pepper, indigo, sandalwood and ambergris from Zanzibar; and fine horses and incense made from tree sap near Aden. It was lists of exotica such as these which attracted Christopher Columbus and which appear in the marginal notes he made in his copy of Marco Polo's book (which he sent to London for in 1498).[1]

One of the longer passages concerning the all-important spices is that describing the surprising quantities of pepper brought daily into Hangzhou on China's eastern coast. Polo declares he heard from a customs official that every single day 43 cartloads of pepper were brought to the city, each cartload containing 223 lb.[2] Even allowing that Hangzhou's markets presumably served a far greater populace than the city's one million inhabitants but dividing by the fact that pepper (if pepper was what he meant) was hardly used in the cuisine of the area, it was still a lot of pepper.

Pepper, and other spices such as cinnamon, cloves, ginger and nutmeg, were the oriental products most essential to medieval Europe. Together with related items such as scented woods and dyestuffs, they were impossible to grow in the more temperate climate of Europe and thus remained a Far Eastern monopoly, carried westwards mainly by sea. Interruptions to the spice trade meant that, on occasion, spices reached such high prices that they were used in payment instead of silver or gold.[3]

Aside from spices, which were a virtual necessity, Far Eastern luxury items were also appreciated in Europe, and of these silk was the most significant. Prized in ancient Rome, its production remained mysterious, the poet Virgil perpetuating the notion that it was combed from the leaves of trees.[4] Even after the Emperor Justinian received smuggled silkworm cocoons at Constantinople in AD 552, it took another hundred years or so before the mysteries of raising silkworms and reeling the filament were unravelled and production was established in the Near East.[5] In Europe, silk production took longer to develop, and the material and its production remained somewhat mysterious. James I of England issued an edict in 1608 promoting the cultivation of mulberries (to provide leaves for the feeding of silkworms) but with little result. One Englishman started a moth farm, but discovered eventually that he was rearing the wrong kind of moth; and it was not until the late seventeenth century with the arrival of Huguenot refugees in Spitalfields that the English silk industry really took off.[6]

With such misapprehensions, it is not surprising that local production did not immediately supply the demand for silks. Far Eastern silks continued to be brought to Europe, mainly by the overland route organised by Persian middlemen, until the development of direct European trade via sea routes in the sixteenth century. Fashions changed, for whilst the decadent Romans seem to have favoured diaphanous Chinese silks, thirteenth-century Europeans preferred heavier damasks woven in the Near East; however it was still worth trading in the finer Chinese silk because of the profit that could be made.[7] Thus, although silk remained secondary to spices in the impetus to explore, it still provided a considerable incentive.

In the context of trade with the East, and Venetian trade in particular, the Polos were well placed. Marco the Elder (uncle of Marco the Traveller) had a house in Constantinople and a house in Soldaia (or Sudak) on the Crimean coast of the Black Sea. (In his will [1280] he left the Crimean house to the Franciscan order – '*dimitto fratribus minoribus*' – though he wanted his son and daughter to carry on living there.[8]) Spices and silks were not traded through Soldaia, though furs of all sorts were brought there by Russian traders; nevertheless, it was a major entrepôt between West and East.

In the prologue to the *Description of the World*, the first trip of Maffeo and Niccolo Polo was from their other base in Constantinople, where they loaded themselves with jewels and proceeded to Soldaia and then 'further afield'. On the long journey out to the Far East, whether by land or sea, 'trading on' was the normal method. This form of trade – taking goods to the first entrepôt, selling them there and buying fresh goods for the next stop – was practised by individual merchants and larger enterprises such as the East India Companies (from the sixteenth century). This was done partly because, with the exception of the goods noted above, most markets were fairly restricted in scope, preferring known articles produced not far away.[9] This method had the advantage of ensuring a return on the original investment. Taking a new cargo to a relatively unknown destination where it might not have been welcome could have meant a loss of the whole sum invested in the venture. By continually selling and buying such a major loss could be avoided. The problem of interesting people in unknown products was encountered by the Macartney embassy to China (1792–94), which took the most up-to-date scientific instruments to the Chinese court, hoping to impress and create a market, but found the instruments dismissed as gadgets and toys by none other than the Emperor himself.[10] In taking jewels, which were light, luxury items of international interest, the Polos could be sure of future sales.

Apart from the description of the elder Polos' movements in the *Description of the World* and the mention of houses in the entrepôts of Sudak and Constantinople in the will of Marco the Elder, there are a few other surviving documents which indicate the Polo family's trade connections. These are mostly related to legal disputes and indicate that, despite the legendary wealth of the Polos, they were in fact small merchants, depositing a small sum of money with a local artisan Alberto Vasirulo and trading spices with Paolo Girardo in 1316. Another document describes how two Polos,

Stefano and Giovanni, sons of Niccolo, then trading in Crete, were shipwrecked and lost 4,000 ducats.[11]

Apart from the occasional reference to disputes with other merchants, the family does not seem to have made a mark on Venice. This is not necessarily surprising. The thirteenth-century merchants of Genoa and Venice seem to have been extremely careful not to commit their plans to paper, presumably for fear of competition. Most foreign trade was governed by the *colleganza* system in Venice, a form of contract between the traveller, who provided a third of the required investment, and an associate, who remained behind though providing two-thirds of the funds required, with the eventual profits being equally divided.[12] These contracts are bare of descriptive detail and the later merchants' handbook, Pegolotti's *Pratica della Mercatura* (*c.* 1340), which is often measured against the *Description of the World*, was written not by a trader, but by a banker. Pegolotti worked for the Florentine Company of the Bardi in Antwerp, London, Cyprus and Ayas, travelling no further east than the Holy Land, but apparently managing to gather his information on the details of travel in the more distant Far East through conversations with those who had actually made the journey.[13]

Although the Polos are nowhere mentioned, there are scattered references to other Italian traders in China in various travellers' accounts. John of Montecorvino (1247–1328), Bishop of Peking, described a merchant, Petrus de Lucalongo, who travelled with him from Tabriz to Peking in 1291 and who later provided funds to build the first Catholic cathedral in Peking. In 1305, John of Montecorvino sent his first letter to the Pope from Karakorum via un-named Venetian merchants who were returning home, protected in the Mongol domains by a golden safe-conduct tablet or 'passport'.[14]

One of the most tantalising monuments to Italian trade with China is the tombstone of a young Italian girl found in Yangzhou in 1951. She died in 1342, but her tombstone was moved in the late fifteenth century to build the walls of the city. In Gothic script inscribed on marble, she was named as Katerina, daughter of Domenico de Vilioni, apparently from a family that had been trading in Tabriz in the mid-thirteenth century. The elaborate tombstone, with its carved Madonna depicted above scenes of the martyrdom of the virgin Saint Catherine being sliced by wheels fitted with knives, suggests that she was not a tiny baby when she died and some authorities assume that her father pre-deceased her.[15] The presence of a Franciscan convent in Yangzhou in the 1320s (mentioned by Odoric of Pordenone[16]) may well explain the design of the tombstone, though most agree that its style suggests that it was actually made by local Chinese artisans. Nevertheless, it remains a mysterious testament to the travels of Italian silk merchants.

In the light of seventeenth- and eighteenth-century European trade with China, when no foreign women were allowed on the mainland,[17] the presence of a daughter and her tombstone is surprising.

However, the armchair guidebook writer Pegolotti, who wrote specifically for travelling merchants, recommended that they should take women along with them, presumably to provide comfort, although he seemed to suggest that one should choose women who know the local languages, which would not, presumably, include daughters commemorated in Latin.[18]

The family name of the young girl, Vilioni, has led to some confusion, for a possible ancestor of Katerina's, Johannes Vilioni, is also referred to as Johannes Milion in a document dated 1185;[19] and since Marco Polo was occasionally referred to as '*il milioni*',[20] there have been suggestions that they were related. However there seems to be nothing, apart from a spelling variation, to link the Genoese and the Venetian.

That the tombstone was erected in Yangzhou is also

interesting because Marco Polo is said to have claimed to have governed the city for three years,[21] some forty or fifty years before Katerina's death. Whilst there is absolutely no record of Marco Polo in the Yangzhou gazetteers, there is equally no mention of other resident Italian merchants and their families. The position of the Polos amongst these other merchants is based entirely upon the description given in the Prologue to the *Description of the World*. No trace remains of the Polos in Yangzhou and it is perhaps to be regretted that none of them died there, for a handsome tombstone would have been useful.

Despite the scanty evidence of the sojourn of Italian merchants, the Mongols were clearly less concerned with keeping out foreigners than later Chinese rulers. Their frequent use of non-Mongol and non-Chinese experts is well known, and their control through family branches of most of Asia meant that travel was generally less restricted than at other times. That they allowed foreign Christians to build cathedrals in Chinese cities and reside there (Italian bishops lived in Quanzhou from 1313 for a decade and at Peking from 1307–28) also indicates a lack of insularity, which obviously extended to the free travel of merchants in the silk-producing areas around Yangzhou.

3

Missionaries
nose to tail

Though the Prologue to the *Description of the World* makes it
clear that the elder Polos arrived in Karakorum as merchants, they left as Christian ambassadors, bearing a letter
to the Pope (which has not been preserved) and promis-
ing to return with various religious tokens. Their apparent
self-transformation from merchants to missionary messengers reflects the importance of religious communication
between East and West and the widespread desire to know
more about the spiritual situation beyond medieval Europe.

These aims were of such significance to the Christian
rulers of Europe that it sometimes seems that medieval
missionary travellers were practically nose to tail across Central Asia. Though Marco Polo's *Description of the World* is the
best-known medieval account of Mongolia and China, it is
amazing how many missionary documents survive. There
are letters in Persian and Mongol from the Mongol Khans
preserved in the Vatican and the French National Archives[1]
and eyewitness accounts of parts of Mongolia and, eventually, China, written by a variety of Christian missionary
envoys between the mid-thirteenth and early fourteenth centuries; and in the official history of the Mongol era (*Yuan
shi*), the first European to be mentioned by name was John
of Marignolli, a papal envoy to the Khans between 1330

and 1340. His own memoirs, written on his return, were described as 'the work of an incoherent and not very intelligent old man, and . . . in atrocious Latin'.[2]

The most compelling reasons for Christian rulers in Europe to make contact with the Mongols on the other side of the world were contradictory. The various crusades undertaken between 1096 and 1270 had begun as military missions to protect the pilgrimage routes to the Holy City of Jerusalem and ended as more straightforward military attempts to retake parts of the Holy Land which had been firmly occupied by various Muslim rulers. Faced with the strength of Muslim rule, Christian leaders contemplated possible alliances with Mongol rulers whose homeland lay beyond the Muslim strongholds. At the same time, there was a more nervous 'fact-finding' aspect to these tentative approaches to the Mongols, for they had shown themselves to be as effective as the Muslims in empire-building. In 1242 Mongol armies had reached the gates of Vienna; thus Christian rulers were contemplating alliance with a people that appeared to be threatening their very existence. By the time that the Polos set off on their second journey to the East, three major areas of Mongol control were already established under three khanates, that of 'the West' or the Golden Horde, which covered much of European Russia, the Levant, which reached from Eastern Persia to the Mediterranean, and the Central Asian Chaghatai khanate in Turkestan.

In sending missionaries to the Mongols, Popes and Christian rulers alike were influenced by rumours of the existence of a 'Christian' ruler on the eastern edge of the world, Prester John. It was felt that he, perhaps, might be willing to come to the aid of those defending Christendom against Islam. The earliest Christian missionaries, armed with papal letters and charged with finding Christian converts and potential allies amongst the Mongols, arrived in Karakorum some time before the Polos made their first and far better known trip eastward.

The first lengthy account of Mongolia and the Mongols was given by the Franciscan friar John of Plano Carpini (or Pian di Carpini), who was sent by Pope Innocent IV 'into the north-east parts of the world in the year of our Lord 1246'.[3] Plano Carpini, described by a friend as being so fat that he had to ride a very sturdy donkey rather than a horse,[4] came from the small town, Pian di Carpini, near Perugia, and was a disciple of the great St Francis of Assisi (*c.* 1182–1226). His first long trip was a diplomatic mission to Russia, where he was sent by Innocent IV to try to bring the Russian Church to acknowledge papal supremacy, and thus form a 'Catholic anti-Mongol bloc'.[5] For the Russians this was a delicate matter, as much of their territory from the Volga to the Dnieper was already part of the Mongol bloc, and thus in no position to join any anti-Mongol opposition. Qinghis' grandson Batu had, by 1240, taken the Volga area known to the Russians as the Khanate of the Golden Horde. David Morgan says that the name was 'possibly a reference to the Khan's tent' (the golden part) but, in a linguistic loan, 'horde' is derived from the Turkish term 'ordu' meaning camp. The contemporary meaning of 'horde' owes nothing to tents but refers to a large, unruly gathering, arising from and reflecting the way that the Russians and others to the west felt about the devastating army that swept inexorably through the countryside.[6] From Batu's camp, the fat Friar John rode on his donkey across the Altai mountains towards Karakorum. There, Güyüg was camped outside the city. The huge assembly of Mongol princes gathered to elect him as Khan in succession to his father, Ögedei, was just about to take place (August 1246) and Mongols and ambassadors were accommodated in a large tent city put up for the occasion.

Güyüg sent Friar John back with a negative letter to the Pope but, as with many early diplomatic missions to the Far East, John's diplomatic failure was matched by an impressive achievement in his detailed account of Mongol life and customs. Numerous manuscript copies survive in Latin and Friar John's account was included in the compilation made by Vincent de Beauvais (1190–1264), the *Speculum Historiae* (1244). (This was a history of the world from the Creation to the thirteenth century, though the author, described as the greatest of compilers, was said to lack a critical spirit in his approach to the material included.[7])

A fuller account of the Mongols was made by the first missionary to actually get inside the city of Karakorum. William of Rubruck was a Franciscan Friar who accompanied King Louis IX of France on his crusade in the Holy Land, which set out in 1248 (though William may have joined up later). William of Rubruck travelled via Soldaia and Constantinople (like the elder Polos some years later) and reached Karakorum (which he famously compared unfavourably with St Denis, near Paris) in 1254. Although he carried a letter from the French King to the Mongol ruler, Friar William seems to have been most interested in preaching the Gospel to the Mongols.[8]

His account of his travels and descriptions of Mongol life survives in five manuscripts and for its pioneering observation was partially incorporated in the *Opus Maius* of Roger Bacon (*c.* 1220–92). Bacon argued that knowledge of the world's creator was best achieved through exact measurement and observation of the world like William of Rubruck's observations of Mongolia. Despite Bacon's accolade it has been suggested that the unofficial nature of the mission meant that Friar William's account was less widely circulated than Friar John's,[9] which is to be regretted since William's account is fuller and more personal. He described the city of Karakorum, its temples, markets, separate quarters for Muslims and Chinese handicraft workers and its wall in some detail[10] where Marco Polo only wrote, 'Caracorom is a city which is all of timber and earth which in my judgement is three miles round.'[11] The Polo account, disappointingly brief, continues in some versions with an account of a 'very large castle' outside the city. This reference, considered 'obscure' by one commentator,[12] could perhaps be a confusion with or version of the encampment visited by Friar John of Plano Carpini, the temporary 'city of tents' erected to honour the appointment of the new Khan in 1246. William of Rubruck's account, however is a full diary, telling of the people he met including his hopelessly drunk interpreter, the French goldsmith Boucher and his wonderful silver wine-dispensing tree, the goldsmith's near-death from the administration of rhubarb by an Armenian priest, meals provided by a woman from Lorraine, and William's endless quarrels with the Nestorian priests.

The two first Franciscans sent on papal orders, rather than those of the King of France, got no further than Mongolia but another member of the same Order, John of Montecorvino (1247–1328), arrived in Peking in 1291, when the Polos might well have been in China, even in Peking. He built his first church in Peking, complete with bell tower, in 1299, and organised choirs of little boys to sing hymns for the Khan. John of Montecorvino wrote letters describing his work (and its difficulties) but left no descriptive account of the country. His letters testify to the comings and goings of Italians such as Petrus of Lucalongo, who provided funds for the second church in Peking in 1305, and the less welcome 'Lombard leech and chirurgeon' who spread blasphemies about the Church and Rome around Peking in 1302.[13]

Odoric of Pordenone, a Franciscan monk, whose title suggests Italian connections but who, I discovered in Prague, is claimed as a local hero as he was of Bohemian origin, travelled to China between 1320 and 1330, and many manuscripts of his account of his journey survive. He visited China and India later than the Polos but travelled to many of the same places. Odoric's journey was eventful. Whilst in India he gathered the bones of four Franciscan martyrs who had been trying to establish a mission on the Malabar coast. He intended to take them home for burial, but, finding himself becalmed and despairing on his way to China by sea, he threw a martyr's skull into the water waves: a wind immediately sprang up and blew the ship onwards to Canton. There he said he saw enormous geese, like those weighing twenty-four pounds described by Marco Polo in Fujian province (a little further up the coast). Both writers describe the jowls and protuberances on the heads of these monstrous fowl.[14] Odoric noted fishing cormorants and women with bound feet and, when in Yangzhou, described the Franciscan house there (whose fathers were presumably responsible for the design of Katherine of Vilione's tombstone).

Despite the apparent accuracy of much of his account, Odoric of Pordenone could not resist describing mysterious lands of pygmies and the 'vegetable lamb'.

> Another passing marvellous thing that may be related, which however I saw not myself, but heard from trustworthy persons. For 'tis said . . . there be mountains . . . on which are said to grow certain very large melons. And when these be ripe, they burst, and a little beast is found inside like a small lamb, so that they have both melons and meat! And though some, peradventure, may find that hard to believe, yet it may be quite true; just as it is true that there be in Ireland trees which produce birds.[15]

Though Odoric himself accepted that some might be sceptical about the melon, the historian Sir Henry Yule exercised himself to demonstrate that the reference is to the fern genus *Cibotium* or *Aspidium baromez*, whose rhizomes are covered with a white silky down and have a reddish interior which could resemble a small furry beast. Yule did not discuss the edibility of the fern (many are poisonous) and admitted the problem of the distance between the home of the fern (the Volga) and China, and lost track of the melons entirely.

Lamb-bearing vegetables aside, the surprising number of

missionary visitors to the mysterious Mongols in Karakorum, and the flow of papal letters and their responses, indicate that, though the Polos were by no means pioneers in European–Mongol contact, their assumption of the role of Christian messengers was appropriate to the times.

4

Prester John
and the Magi

Missionaries and merchants bearing important papal letters
and charged with information-gathering on the Mongols'
military capacity and their social organisation were travelling
into the unknown. From the days of Pliny, who formed
Shakespeare's view of 'cannibals that each other eat, the
Anthropophagi, and men whose heads do grow beneath
their shoulders',[1] the distant lands of the East were not
only strange but terrifying. Interestingly, the Chinese held
parallel views about dwellers in the distant West, who they
thought hopped on one leg or had heads like dogs.[2] Aside
from these legendary monsters, the most important beliefs
for Christian missionaries to Asia were the legends concerning Prester John, and the papal disapproval of the Nestorian
schism, which was a political, rather than a superstitious
question. Nestorian Christians from the Lebanon and Persia
are significant for they may have acted as interpreters for
the missionaries as well as, perhaps, the Polos, through their
knowledge of Persian, Arabic, Latin and Mongol.

Prester John has now been sited in Africa, thanks to Rider
Haggard and John of Marignolli (mid fourteenth century)
who set his domain in Ethiopia,[3] but in the thirteenth
century he was thought to be a pious Christian ruler of the
Far East. The beginning of the legend appears to arise from

a visit to Rome in 1122 of an Eastern priest. Nothing is known of his background though he claimed to have come from India and told of the miracles that occurred there every year on the feast of St Thomas. This led many to believe that Prester John ruled in India. (St Thomas was believed to have gone to India to preach after the crucifixion and his activities there were recorded in the apocryphal Acts of Thomas, apparently written in Syriac in Edessa in the early third century.[4]) Some twenty years after the mysterious Indian priest's visit, the Prester John legend was complicated by news of a defeat of Muslims in Central Asia by a Nestorian priest-king. Bishop Otto of Freisingen (who was probably confusing a Chinese victory over Muslim forces near Samarkand in 1141) said that he heard this news from the Bishop of Gabala (in Syria), whom he had met in Viterbo.[5] The Bishop of Gabala also reported the heartening news that Prester John had been trying to come and help the Crusaders but had been held up.[6] Prester John was also said to be a descendant of one of the Three Wise Men or Magi. Others suggest that Prester John was a version of Yelu dashi, a Khitan general who had fled China for Central Asia in 1125 when the Jin dynasty overthrew the Khitan Liao rulers of North China. Like many, including later Mongol Khans, Yelu dashi seems to have been surrounded by Nestorian clerics, Christians deemed heretical by the papacy in Rome.

The Prester John legend grew when a letter (which still survives), addressed to the Byzantine emperor Manuel I Comnenus (1143–80) and purporting to come from Prester John, began to circulate in Europe in 1156. The letter describes Prester John as ruling in India, from the Tower of Babel to the land where the sun rises.[7] The letter, by an 'anonymous forger', prompted Pope Alexander III to send his doctor on a mission to meet Prester John, but the doctor seems to have been lost in Palestine in 1177. Despite this setback, the belief in a Christian ruler who might help defend the Holy Land against the Muslims continued to offer hope to the Crusaders.

Marco Polo's account of Prester John downplayed the Christian aspect, but described how Qinghis Khan wanted to marry Prester John's daughter and killed John in battle when refused (though in one manuscript version of the *Description of the World*, Qinghis Khan subsequently married the daughter anyway[8]). This story was first set down in the account of Friar Julian, a Hungarian Dominican who reported on his travels on the fringe of the Mongol empire in 1236; it is said to have been a common story in Western and Central Asia at the time.[9]

Polo sited Prester John's kingdom on the eastern edge of Inner Mongolia[10] and stated that it was the land we call 'Gog and Magog'.[11] He did not mention the view held by Arab geographers that Gog and Magog were giants who had been walled up by Alexander the Great and that their wall, in turn, was often held to be the Chinese Great Wall,[12] parts of which lie in the area in which Marco Polo set Prester John's kingdom. Polo also stated that Prester John's realm was that ruled by his grandson, George. This is a strange mixing of reality with legend for George, a real person (but apparently the grandson of a legendary being), was the ruler of the Ongut, a tribe that had long embraced Nestorianism. George himself was converted to Roman Catholicism by John of Montecorvino in the last years of the thirteenth century.[13]

Conversion of Nestorians (even if their antecedents were glorious but non-existent) was a major pre-occupation of papal missionaries. The Nestorian Church was a great irritant. Virtually unknown today, the Nestorian Christian Church, reviled as heretical by orthodox churchmen like the Franciscan William of Rubruck, was very strong in the east, overlapping with and extending eastward beyond the Islamic world at the time that the Polos travelled to Mongolia.

Nestorianism began with the beliefs of Nestorius, who was Bishop of Constantinople from 428 to 431, when he was dismissed for his heresy. He clashed with Cyril, Patriarch of Alexandria, over the divinity of Christ. Cyril emphasised Christ's divinity whilst Nestorius used a strikingly modern argument to dismiss the divinity of Mary, arguing that she was only mother of Christ 'in his humanity', and stressed also the human nature of Christ. Later Nestorians abhorred representations of the crucifixion (perhaps because of the human suffering depicted) and frequently sabotaged William of Rubruck's attempts to produce crucifixes and other Christian images for the Mongol Court of Karakorum.

Nestorian Christians were largely responsible for the veneration of St Thomas in India, maintaining his shrine near Madras, which Marco Polo is credited with being the first to describe,[14] although unfortunately he described nothing except coconuts and miracles, the latter well-known (much curing of the sick and lame and causing rich misers to repent).[15] John of Montecorvino also said almost nothing about the shrine although he spent thirteen months in the region at roughly the same time as the Polos, but this is probably because of his dislike of (and determination to poach and convert) Nestorians.[16]

The need to coexist with Nestorians, despite the difficulty of their schismatic beliefs, arose partly out of their position of power and closeness to various of the Central Asian rulers. It may also have been more basic: as Nestorian monks were familiar with the languages of the East and the routes across Asia, they may have served as interpreters to many travellers. Ascelinus, sent by Pope Innocent IV in 1248 to the Mongols in Armenia, returned with an escort including a Nestorian priest with whom he does not seem to have got on at all.[17] It is hard to imagine that papal envoys travelled alone in these difficult areas, and the widely travelled and widely established Nestorians would have been obvious interpreters; though in the case of the Franciscans, for example, conscious of religious differences, their necessary reliance upon 'heretics' must have been galling.

Marco Polo also made two confusing contributions to know-ledge about Christianity in the Near and Far East. First, he managed to track down the supposed homeland of the Three Kings. In Persia, he visited the town from which the Three Magi were said to have set out, though the present inhabitants could only tell him that they were former kings of the area and how, bringing back a stone which produced fire, they gave rise to the fire-worshipping cult of Zoroastrianism in the area.[18] The fact that the three travellers who are so closely associated with the birth of Christ apparently introduced a completely different new religion in Persia may have been confusing to those who read his book closely.

Polo's other great discovery on behalf of Christianity was a group of terrified believers in Fuzhou, capital of the southern province of Fujian in China. They did not worship fire (and were therefore not Zoroastrians) or idols (and were therefore not Buddhists), but nor did they, according to a local 'Saracen' informer, worship either Mahomet or Christianity. However, after some difficult translation work, the Polos identified their holy book as the Psalter and informed them that they were indeed Christians.[19] However, most scholars now believe that 'Marco Polo and his uncle had stumbled upon a group of Manichaeans',[20] for the church is known to have existed in Fujian province, near Quanzhou, but not necessarily in Fuzhou. The Manichaeans did, apparently, include a form of the Psalter amongst their religious books, but the three images on the altar, identified by the Polos as three of the apostles, are thought to have been a common Chinese Buddhist trinity (Amitabha, Avalokitesvara or Guanyin, and Mahasthama, the 'three holy ones of the Western region'), borrowed by the eclectic Manichaeans.[21] Manichaeism developed from the teachings of Mani (*c.* 276 BC to *c.* 216 BC), who drew on the Persian fire-worshipping religion of Zoroastrianism, but whose followers also embraced aspects of Buddhism and Christianity, thus developing a dualistic view of the world. Manichaeism stressed the opposition between God and the light, bright, spiritual world, and Satan and the dark, material world. Humans were thought to contain both aspects but could strive to achieve greater lightness and spirituality by asceticism, vegetarianism, pacificism and celibacy (for women were evil, binding men to the flesh). Manichaeism, with its Zoroastrian (light, fire) and Buddhist (ascetic, pacific) aspects, may seem foreign to us now, but St. Augustine was a 'manichee' for nine years (though later condemning the religion) and its dualist views were seen as persisting in later heresies such as those of the Bogomils and the Albigensians or Cathars, thorns in the flesh of the orthodox European Church during the Middle Ages.[22]

A problem with Marco Polo's identification of the Manichaeans as Christians is that the passage occurs only in the fifteenth-century 'Toledo' manuscript. Other traces of Manichaeans in Fujian province include the more concrete evidence of a tombstone found in Quanzhou and a nearby shrine, so their existence is not to be doubted; but whether Marco Polo saw them himself is more questionable as the Toledo manuscript contains other passages not found in any other early versions of the *Description of the World* and which may have been later additions to the text.

Whoever wrote it, the passage relating to the Manichaeans as Christians testifies to the desire of medieval Europeans to see Christians in the Far East, as does the legend of Prester John. The spread of Christianity and the consequent possibility of forging links with Christians in distant parts of the world (as long as they were not Nestorians) were not only a spur to missionary travel to the Far East but a matter of strong interest to medieval readers, who would have been comforted by the episodes included in various versions of the *Description of the World*.[23]

5

Not an itinerary

While the religious detail given in the *Description of the World* sets it firmly in its time, against the background of Christian overtures to the Mongols, the descriptions of products from all the countries of the Near East, the Far East and South-East Asia reveal Europe's growing merchantile interest in exotic spices and fabrics. These details are described after the Prologue, which sets the background of the Polos' travels against which the remainder of the tale is seen. Yet despite the fact that popular versions of Marco Polo's book are often entitled '*The Travels*', a close reading of the text beyond the Prologue does not provide a logical itinerary. It moves roughly from West to East and back again, but in geographical chunks, not as the diary of a journey. Though expeditions continue to be mounted 'in the footsteps of Marco Polo', distinguished travellers, when closely questioned, admit that it is not actually possible to follow Marco Polo step by step beyond Persia.[1]

The main body of the text begins with a shifting chronicle of the Middle East, offering descriptions of produce, the inhabitants and their beliefs, but no record of the Polos' movement from one city to the next. Indeed, it is much closer to a general geography than a travel record. There are mentions of distances – 'You should know that from

Baghdad to the sea is a journey of fully eighteen days',[2] 'The traveller who leaves this city [Yazd] to proceed further rides for fully seven days over a plain in which there are only three inhabited places where he can get shelter'[3] – but these are offered as they might appear in a general guidebook. (A trip from from Baghdad to the sea would, at this stage, have turned the Polos back towards home prematurely.)

In Central Asia, the cities are described in a possible sequence: Yarkand, Khotan, Pem, Charchan, Lop, and Shazhou, before a sudden digression to the north – 'Now I will tell you of some of the cities which lie towards the north-west near the edge of this desert'[4] – after which digression the reader is taken back to Shazhou, before turning due north for the Mongol capital of Karakorum and onwards to the north to 'the ocean'. (Which ocean is not specified though the direction suggests north of Siberia.) The text then doubles back to Ganzhou and starts again, this time north-east to Shangdu (Xanadu). A digression on Qubilai Khan follows, with a description of Peking and details of banquets, hunting and a famous account of the Chinese postal system where, in the Turkestan area, Chinese postmen used dogs to pull the post-sleighs.[5]

Within China, there is a lack of dates although the sections are, as with the Near East and Central Asia, generally arranged in a geographical manner, with some details given of the time taken to get from one city to the next: 'From Taiyuanfu, seven days' ride towards the west [south, actually] . . . will bring you to Pingyangfu.'[6] The rough direction is generally south-west, across the Yellow River, past Chengdu in Sichuan province, to the Yangtse and on into Tibet. After Tibet comes Yunnan and the Burmese border. After Burma, Bengal. Retracing his steps, the traveller must be assumed to have made his weary way back to Peking from Bengal before beginning another trail, along the eastern seaboard through Nanjing, Suzhou, Yangzhou, Hangzhou to Fujian province, the description of which terminates suddenly, 'We shall now pass on and make our way into India.'[7]

Examining the distances between places (where he could determine which places were which), Sir Henry Yule, working at the end of the nineteenth century when means of transport in China were still very much the same as they were in the thirteenth century (although postmen had abandoned dog-transport), was faced with constant problems. On the possibility of getting from Yongzhang to the Burmese capital in seventeen and a half days, 'I confess that the indications in this and the beginning of the following chapter are, to me, full of difficulty.'[8] Between Burma and Laos he is forced to conclude, 'I do not believe . . . that Polo is now following a route which he had traced in person',[9] and further on he notes reluctantly, 'We are obliged, indeed, to give up the attempt to keep a line of communicating rivers throughout the whole twenty-four days. Nor do I see how it is possible to adhere to that condition literally without taking material liberties with the text.'[10]

After a digression on the ill-fated Mongol sea attack on Japan, apparently entirely based on hearsay, the journey (still described in impersonal terms) takes 'the traveller' from Vietnam to Java, the Andaman islands, Ceylon, India (and St Thomas), then back to Ceylon, back to India and then to the Arabian sea and the two mysterious islands, the Island of Men and the Island of Women, where geography makes way for folklore, Socotra, Madagascar, Zanzibar, Abyssinia and Aden. The cities of Southern Arabia and Persia (Hormuz and Kirman) are described before another sudden change of tack and covering of traces, 'Since we went out by another route . . . we will not loiter here now, but will go on to talk of Turkestan . . .'[11] Long descriptions of Tartar wars and a description of Russia follow and then the book ends abruptly.

The return journey, which one might expect to find rounding off the text but which in fact appears only in the

31

Prologue, apparently took the Polos to the Persian Gulf, via Sumatra. Accompanying the high-born Mongol lady who intended to marry Arghun, they made their way to Tabriz. After they had rid themselves of her, they travelled on horseback to Trabzon and sailed onwards to Constantinople and Venice, arriving there in 1295.

One of the interesting aspects of the *Description of the World* is that this account of the bringing of the princess to Persia from China, only to find that her proposed husband had died, occurs also in the *World History* of Rashīd al-Dīn, written in 1306–7 as a commission from the Ilkan, Ghazan, who married the princess.[12] The story is also told in an official Chinese text included in an imperial manuscript encyclopaedia, *Yongle dadian* (22,877 sections, compiled between 1403 and 1408). For some Chinese historians, the fact that the tale of Arghun and his bride-to-be is included in official Chinese documents is important evidence of Marco Polo's credibility.[13] The only problem with this exciting find is that no mention is made either in the Chinese, or in Rashīd's account, of any Europeans or Italians accompanying the princess. This omission is traditionally explained in two ways. Either Marco Polo was exaggerating his importance as a servant of the Great Khan Qubilai or Rashīd al-Dīn was demonstrating the normal Muslim prejudice against Europeans.[14] However, it could also be argued the story was borrowed from another source.

Looking at the text as a whole, apart from its not being an itinerary, the second thing that I found very surprising is that, beyond the Prologue, it contains remarkably few references to the Polos themselves: it is much more of a geographical or historical work than a personal account of things seen.

Chapter 1, 'The Middle East',[15] which opens, 'Let me begin with Armenia',[16] contains only three references to Marco Polo. The first occurs in a long passage on Persia, which describes the Three Magi from the Bible setting out from Saveh, when 'Messer Marco asked several of the inhabitants who these Magi were; but no one could tell him anything except that they were three kings who were buried there in days gone by'.[17] The second follows an account of the origins of fire-worship in the gift of a stone by the Christ-child to the Three Magi: 'this was related to Messer Marco Polo by the inhabitants of this town';[18] and the third follows an account of the maurauding Kauarunas of Rudbar: 'I assure you that Messer Marco himself narrowly evaded capture by these robbers,'[19] which suggests a chance missed for an exciting tale.

Chapter 2, 'The road to Cathay', similarly contains three references to the Polos, one of which contains the only indication that the 'I' narrator could be Marco Polo. The first possibly refers to an illness suffered by Marco Polo, for 'Messer Marco vouches . . . from his own experience'[20] that the pure air of Balashan (where Alexander's horse Bucephalus served the local mares) is sufficient to cure disease without recourse to medicine. The second introduces a mysterious travelling companion: 'I had a Turkish companion named Zurficar, a man of great intelligence, who spent three years in this province, in the service of the Great Khan, engaged in the extraction of . . . salamander and ond-anique[21] and steel and other products'.[22] In the medieval bestiary, the salamander, a newt-like amphibian, could resist fire and, in an explanation which rushes backwards and forwards between salamanders and asbestos, we are told that 'men spoke of it, and still do, as a beast; but this is not true', for it is 'stuff' dug out of the mountain, which when crumbled and made into cloths, emerges unscathed, indeed, cleansed, by fire.[23] The third reference in Chapter 2 mentions that the Polos spent a year in the city of Ganzhou (today's Zhangye in Gansu province), 'but without any experiences worth recording'.[24] The rest of the chapter is taken up with the story of Prester John, and his ultimately fatal relations with Qinghis Khan, and accounts of Mongol habits and encampments which are very similar indeed to those of the missionaries William of Rubruck and John of Plano Carpini.

Chapter 3, 'Kubilai Khan', contains only one mention of the Polos, a reference back to the meeting between Maffeo, Niccolo and the Khan described in the Prologue. The rest of the chapter contains an account of Peking, the customs of the Chinese and the administration of the state.

Chapter 4, 'From Peking to Bengal', takes a different narrative approach. Instead of referring to 'the traveller' and what 'the traveller' might see or find in Central Asia, it begins with the explanation that 'Messer Marco himself was sent by the Great Khan as an emissary towards the west, on a journey fully four months from Khan-balik [Peking]. So we will tell you what he saw on the way, coming and going.'[25] However, after this promisingly personal start, the narrative resumes the familiar pattern of 'the traveller' seeing this and that, or next encountering such and such a town. Marco Polo reappears on page 189 with reference to Bengal and, unusually, assumes the first person: 'In the year 1290, when I, Marco, was at the court of the Great Khan, it [Bengal] had not been conquered.' The rest of the description of Bengal is, again, impersonal. It may be added that if the order of geographical description in this chapter is taken as the itinerary for Marco Polo's fact-finding mission, the trip from Peking to Bengal and back would have taken far longer than four months; even the outward trip would have been difficult to achieve in that time by horse and boat.

Chapter 5, 'From Peking to Amoy', is largely occupied with the things that the impersonal 'traveller' might expect to see and in only one instance refers to Marco Polo: 'Only such cities have been described as I, Marco, passed through on my journey through the province.'[26] Another reference to the idolatry of the inhabitants describes a method of finding things that are lost. The text mentions eighty-four idols, presumably the large groups of *luohans* (Buddhist saints) commonly found in temples, although they normally occur in groups of twelve, eighteen or five hundred, and concentrates on the two figures who were invoked to find lost property. After describing offerings of cloth made to the idols, Marco Polo adds a disingenuous contribution, 'And by this means I, Marco, found a ring that I had lost – but not by making any offering to the idols or paying them homage.'[27]

Chapter 5 does, however, contain some of the few references to the Polos' service in the Great Khan's administration. On Yangzhou: 'Messer Marco Polo himself, who is the subject of this book, governed this city for three years'[28] (though this is not corroborated by Chinese sources). On the siege of Xiangyang: 'Messer Niccolo and Messer Maffeo and Messer Marco declared, "We shall find you a means by which the city will be forced to surrender forthwith" . . . The Messer Niccolo and his brother and son, who had among their retinue a German and a Nestorian Christian who were masters of this art, bade them make two or three manogonels that hurled stones of 300 pounds.'[29]

In the description of Hangzhou, one of China's prettiest cities, set by the great West Lake, and which had been the second capital of the Song dynasty (from 1127 to 1279, when it was taken by the Mongols), Marco Polo is quoted directly on two counts. He first describes a letter sent by 'the queen of the realm' to the Mongol general Bayan who took the province,[30] which is a rather unlikely text, reading, as quoted, like a guidebook to the layout and administration of Hangzhou. Despite its guidebook nature, it is sometimes said to have been meant as a plea to Bayan not to destroy the elegant city. Marco Polo bears out the accuracy of the contents of the mysterious document: 'It is all true as I, Marco Polo, later saw clearly with my own eyes.' He adds later that he was in the town during the taking of a census and that he saw the head of a monstrous fish, 100 paces long and covered by hairs, that had been found stranded during the siege of Hangzhou by Bayan. A census was taken in 1270 and a whale almost 30 metres in length was recorded as being stranded in 1282; but Hangzhou was captured by the Mongols in 1276, so, unless the Polos spent a considerable time in the city and endured the ordeal of its capture, the dates and events are difficult to reconcile.[31]

The last reference to the Polos in China in Chapter 5 is the interesting one that refers to their 'discovery' of a group of Christians in Fuzhou, the group that is now considered to have been Manichaean rather than Christian.

Chapter 6, 'From China to India', is prefaced by the statement at the end of Chapter 5 that 'Messer Marco stayed so long in India and is so well-acquainted with Indian affairs and customs and commerce, that there has scarcely ever been a man better qualified to give a true account of the country.'[32] Chapter 6 contains only one reference to Marco Polo, Indianist without parallel, and this in reference to Sumatra, where 'I myself, Marco Polo, spent five months, waiting for weather that would permit us to continue our voyage',[33] and in two editions goes on to describe living in a fortified stockade.

Chapter 7, 'India', contains one solitary personal reference to Marco Polo in the kingdom of Maabar, where he saw the king himself fall foul of his own rules concerning the repayment of debt.[34] Chapter 8, 'The Arabian Sea', contains no personal reference to the Polos, nor does Chapter 9, 'Northern Regions and Tartar Wars'.

In one fourteenth-century Tuscan version, an epilogue rounds off the book by referring back to the Prologue, which explains the Polos' difficulty in leaving China and the 'happy chance' which led to their departure. It contains nothing new, though it is a perhaps a more elegant finale to the whole collection of tales than occurs elsewhere.

The non-involvement of the Polos in the narrative, apart from the Prologue and the few mentions cited, leaves an impersonal tone with a strong flavour of the guidebook. Places are described, not in the logical sequence of an itinerary, but in a rough geographical grouping. Within the section on Persia, cities are described in general terms: 'Cobinan (Kuh-banan) is a large city whose inhabitants worship Mahomet and they make large and beautiful mirrors and "tucia", which is very good for eye diseases.'[35]

> From there one travels twelve [Latham has three] days and comes to a city called Taychan (Talikhan) where good grain is sold in the market. It is in a pretty country and the mountains to the South are high and entirely made of salt and all sorts of people make thirty-day journeys to get there. It is the best [salt] in the world but so hard you need a pick to get at it . . . the mountains are also abundant in almonds and pistachios which are sold in quantity in the market.[36]

In Armenia, in a city called Arcinga (Erzincan), is the best buckram (*bucheranj*) in the world,[37] near Basra 'the best dates in the world grow' (*meliores nascuntur datuli qui reperaintur in mundo*) and most of the pearls imported into Christendom from India are pierced in Baghdad (*omnes peruli que de yndia in xristianitem portantur in maiori partte perforantur in baldac*).[38]

These descriptions of luxury goods, their sources and processes were presumably the inspiration for Italo Calvino's *Invisible Cities*, where the mournful Qubilai Khan, depressed by the evening shadows and 'the odour of the elephants after rain', listens to Marco Polo's accounts of thin cities, trading cities and hidden cities, preferring the 'fabulous' tales of the Venetian to the more sober accounts of other travellers who list tons of salt, distances and other dull details.[39]

Unfortunately, those who actually read the *Description of the World* will discover that much of Marco Polo's account of the East does consist of tons of salt and distances. Though these descriptions are sometimes intermingled with stories about Caliphs and Magi, they are fundamentally practical and, even without following a logical itinerary, the book serves more as a merchant's view of the world than that of a creative writer.

6

The ghost writer
and the first fan

One explanation of why Marco Polo's *Description of the World* is a somewhat impersonal travel book, despite the popular title, is buried in the Prologue. The *Description of the World* is always credited to Marco Polo; no other name appears on any title page, so at first glance there is no way of knowing that it was actually ghost written by a popular romance writer of the time. This information is given in the Prologue, which states that 'in the year of the nativity of Our Lord Jesus Christ 1298, while he was in prison in Genoa, wishing to occupy his leisure as well as to afford entertainment to readers, he caused all these things to be recorded by Messer Rustichello of Pisa, who was in the same prison'.[1]

Rustichello, known, at least to the French at the time, as a native of Pisa, was apparently taken prisoner in 1284 at the sea battle of La Meloria (named for a small island off the Tuscan coast) between the Pisans and the Genoese. Most of the Genoese prisoners were released from 1298 onwards and it is likely that Rustichello, a Pisan, was also released around that time in exchange for the release of the Genoese prisoners.

Tantalisingly little is known about Rustichello, indeed Sir Walter Scott seemed to think the name was 'imaginary',[2] though Rustichello was known to literary critics of the nineteenth century. Isaac D'Israeli in his now forgotten *Amenities of Literature* (published in London in 1840) described him as a mercenary who celebrated the chivalry of the British court when 'stimulated by largesses and fair chateaux'.[3] The largesses and chateaux had obviously disappeared by 1284 but Rustichello left two surviving 'romances', both concerned with Arthurian legend, as their titles suggest: *Gyron le Courtois avecque la devise des armes de tous les chevaliers de la table Ronde* (the courtier Gyron and all the tales of the Knights of the Round Table) and *Meliadus de Leonnoys; Ensemble plusieurs autres nobles proesses de chevalerie faictes par le Roy Artus, Palamedes et Galliot de Pré* (a group of stories of the chivalrous deeds of King Arthur and other knights of the Round Table).

Rustichello seems to have spent much of his life away from Italy and his two Arthurian romances were written in French, although, as D'Israeli noted, his major foreign association was with the English court, being Edward I's favourite writer. Rustichello is known to have accompanied Prince Edward (later Edward I) on his crusade to Acre (1270–73). Edward I's first language was French, since this was the language of the English court and his mother, Eleanor of Provence, was French. The links between Britain and France at the time were complex; in 1249, when Edward was ten, he was given all of Gascony in south-west France (and at the age of fifteen, he received Ireland and various other places). Eleanor of Provence had quite a collection of romances[4] but her love of books was not, apparently, inherited, for it was reported in 1300 that Edward only possessed one book, an unnamed romance, one hopes by Rustichello.[5]

It seems that when Prince Edward and Rustichello were stuck in Sicily in 1270–1, on their way to the Holy Land, Rustichello borrowed a book about the Arthurian legends from Edward and used it as the basis for his *Meliadus,* whose epilogue suggests that it was written at royal command.[6] In writing about King Arthur (or Roy Artus), Rustichello could have been certain of success, for Edward I visited Glastonbury in 1278 and had the supposed remains of Arthur and Guinevere dug up and reburied in front of a great altar, rather as if they were saints.[7]

The style of Rustichello's Arthurian romances made its way into the *Description of the World*, especially in the Prologue, where the invitation to 'Lords, Emperors and Kings, Dukes and Marquesses, Counts, Knights and townspeople . . .' is identical to the beginning of his own heroic tales. The Italian scholar Benedetto placed many paragraphs of the *Description of the World* and the romances side by side, revealing considerable similarities,[8] and thus it is probable that Rustichello was largely responsible for the style of the work, which may partly account for the often slightly evasive tone of the narrator.

The style of narration is one of the oddest aspects of the work. The text is not told in the first person, as if dictated or told by Marco Polo. Very occasionally there is a personal note – 'I myself have seen this' – but the major part of the text is straightforward description, 'There is a castle', 'there are mountains', 'the people here are idolators' – with an occasional suggestion of a third person assuring us that Marco Polo saw this or that. Much is even more impersonal, describing what 'the traveller' might see by the way. This may well be the result of co-authorship.

It is intriguing to imagine how such a collaboration came about. One of Marco Polo's earliest publishers and fans, Giovanni Battista Ramusio, who died in 1557, suggested that Marco Polo was an impressive raconteur. He discussed the appellation '*il milione*', which was apparently given to Marco during his lifetime (and which is commemorated in the popular name for the Polo family house in Venice, the Corte de Milione), and said that it was because whenever he told of the great wealth of the Mongol Khans, he counted it in millions of gold coins.[9] To Rustichello, Marco Polo's first audience, the menacing and mysterious Mongols were presumably almost unknown, and the Chinese, inventors of silk, equally strange. Though their book is full of strange and wondrous tales and huge quantities, the Prologue stresses the didactic and informative nature of the collaboration undertaken by Marco Polo 'so that others who have not seen and do not know them may learn them'.[10] Nonetheless, such fabulous wealth and magnificent tales of distant places may well have impressed the romance writer to the point that he proposed a collaboration.

Both Rustichello and Marco Polo describe their captivity in a 'dungeon' but the French medieval historian Jacques Heers suggested that Marco Polo, along with other Venetian prisoners 'of rank', was perhaps held under a form of house arrest in a Genoese family home.[11] This form of imprisonment was apparently current at the time and often used prior to prisoner exchanges, so it was in the interests of Genoese families with relatives imprisoned by the Venetians to accept prisoners in the hope of an eventual exchange. This relatively comfortable imprisonment would have made it easier to collaborate on a book, although it does not accord with some of the legends about Marco Polo. The most famous of these is Ramusio's sixteenth-century description of them as returning to Venice clad in tattered Tartar clothes, ragged and unrecognisable, bereft of all possessions save rubies and emeralds sewn into the seams of their tattered garments,[12] but this ragged return is not borne out by a near contemporary, Jacopo da Acqui,[13] who stated that, when imprisoned, Marco Polo sent to his father for his notes and papers to help him compose his book. These books and papers are puzzling for they could hardly have been brought back from the Far East by someone in rags and quite without other luggage.

Either way, Marco Polo was described by his contemporaries as a remarkable teller of tales; indeed, da Acqui suggested that he had only told half of what he knew though he was always ready to list the amazing numbers of bridges, piles of gold coins, cartloads of pepper and warring elephants to anyone who would listen. That Europeans were increasingly curious to read more is evident from the enormous number of surviving manuscripts of the text, though most were produced after Marco Polo's death. The number of texts, however, presents one of the most vexing aspects of Marco Polo's account of the world and his travels. As one expert puts it, these 'exist in most of the languages of Western Europe, not excluding Irish'.[14] Or, perhaps, including Irish.

It is difficult to give a precise number of early surviving copies: 143 different manuscript and printed versions of the text have been identified,[15] with seven separate or related versions. The differences in their status are based on variations in language or dialect used, as some of the Italian dialects are very close. The 'languages' of the different versions include Romance (or Franco-Italian), Court French, Latin, Venetian, Tuscan, German, Spanish, Bohemian, Aragonese, Catalan, Portuguese, Irish (a printed edition of 1460 in the Chatsworth collection) and English (John Frampton's printed edition of 1579). Their dates range from 1351 to the nineteenth century and, though they are traditionally grouped into two major families, originating in French or Latin, many reveal startling differences in content.

It is usually stated that the 'original' manuscript has not survived, for none are 'signed' by the ghost-writer Rustichello or Marco Polo. In all cases of manuscript transmission, there are problems of copyists' errors, which can be repeated or further confused in subsequent copying, and in every written culture there has been a long tradition of palaeographical search for accuracy. In the case of the Polo manuscripts, there are the added problems of the translation from one language to another and of unfamiliar foreign names. These, combined with the lapse of time between the events, the compilation of the work and the earliest surviving versions, have led to the extreme variation in the contents of the 143 or 150 manuscripts.

The earliest dated reference to the text occurs in a note appended to a French manuscript edition destined for Charles de Valois, son of the French King Philip the Fair. The note states that Charles' emissary, Thibault de Chepoy, received the copy from Polo himself in 1307, '*Monseigneur Thybault Chevalier Seigneur de Cepoy... il en eust la coppie a messere Marc Pol bourgeois et habitant en la cite de Venise... Et fut fait l'an de l'incarnation nostre seigneur Jhesu Crist mil trois cent et sept au mois d'aoust*' (Thibault de Chepoy received this copy from Marco Polo, citizen and resident of the city of Venice, in August 1307).[16]

Thibault appears to have had many copies made from his copy, and Benedetto identified one in a collection including other geographical and travellers' texts, such as Sir John Mandeville's *Travels* and the itinerary of Odoric of Pordenone, now in Berne. However, he considered this to be a fifteenth-century manuscript, which would make it a late copy of a copy. Thibault's text is not, however, the version that experts agree to be the 'best' text; that is another Franco-Italian manuscript, written in Italy in the first half of the fourteenth century and now kept in the Bibliothèque Nationale in Paris.[17]

There are two major early groups of texts; the earliest appear to be the Franco-Italian group, which was the source of translations into Court French, Latin, Venetian and Tuscan. Benedetto, who gave the first full account of manuscripts known up to 1928 in his *Il Milione*, provides a significant 'family tree' of manuscripts, where surviving manuscripts are depicted as a third, fourth or fifth generation copy of several lost versions.[18]

The first surviving Latin version was produced by Friar Francesco Pipino from a dialect version, possibly during Marco Polo's lifetime, for Pipino said it was made after 1315 and declared, '*Marchus Paulus Venetus in quondam suo libello a me in Latinum ex vulgari idiomate Lombardico translatum*' (I translated the Venetian Marco Polo's book into Latin from vulgar Lombard).[19] Pipino's translation was one of the most widely circulated versions of the *Description of the World*.

The first promoter of the Polo legend was Giovanni Battista Ramusio, who died in 1557. He insisted that he worked from an early Latin manuscript of the *Description of the World* written in about 1438, but the contents of his published version of the book are quite different from the Pipino version. (Sadly, many of Ramusio's papers appear to have been destroyed in a fire in 1557, so his Latin original is unlikely to appear.)

Ramusio's enthusiasm for Marco Polo arose from his search for books about travel and exploration when he began to compile a collection of these works for publication. His *Navigationi et Viaggi* (*Navigations and Voyages*), including a version of Marco Polo's book, was printed in 1559, two years after his death. It appeared at a time when European voyagers were already beginning to reach distant corners of the world. Christopher Columbus (who carried with him a version of Marco Polo's book as well as other travel writings) had reached America in 1492 and Sir John Frobisher also took travel writings about the world when he explored Baffin Bay in 1576.[20]

Whilst their contemporaries explored the world, it seems that travel writing was beginning to be enjoyed by stay-at-home readers. The English geographer, Richard Hakluyt (*c.*1551–1616), like Ramusio, spent years of his life collecting accounts of travels, which were published in 1589–90 in *The Principal Navigations, Voyages, Traffiques and Discoveries of the English Nation*.[21] It is possible that when Marco Polo and Rusticello embarked upon their collaboration they were anticipating public interest in travel and exploration but, unfortunately for them, passionate interest in travel books appears to have developed about a hundred years too late.

For some 400 years, Ramusio's version of Marco Polo's book remained one of the most lively, for he included stories of Marco Polo and his exaggerated conversation and the romantic version of his return to Venice, told 'in the best Arabian nights manner', where the Polo family failed to ·recognise their ragged relatives 'with a *je ne sais quoi* of the Tartar about them'.[22] Ramusio included many passages that do not appear in any other surviving editions, like the healing girdles of the monks of San Barsamo in Tabriz,[23] the description of the bustling city of Hangzhou and the marriage of Qinghis Khan to Prester John's daughter. This last has to be an impossibility since Prester John was a legendary being and thus his daughter would have to have been equally non-corporeal, and in any case Qinghis' wife was well known, but it is a neat way of rounding off a story of the interminable battles between the Khan and Prester John.[24] True to the exciting nature of the version, one of the most significant sections of the Ramusio version is the lengthy description of Qinghis' palace and his concubines and the method of their selection.[25]

That Ramusio's version, based on a lost Latin manuscript and published over 200 years after Marco Polo's death, is fuller and more interesting than earlier surviving manuscripts is worrying. It seems possible that he incorporated extra material in order to make the work more interesting. Some of what he added, such as the romantic story of the return to Venice, is acceptable as part of the 'legend' of Marco Polo himself, but the insertion of long passages about Qinghis' concubines and lavishly decorated palace into the text itself is more serious. Since the Latin manuscript that he said he used was destroyed, it is impossible to know who wrote these passages, but it seems unlikely that it was Marco Polo or Rustichello. Ramusio probably felt that he was helping his hero by making the book fuller and more interesting.

Ramusio's was not the only version that appeared to have been 'improved'. Another Latin version, apparently translated from Franco-Italian or Romance and copied in the fifteenth century, was discovered in the Cathedral Library of Toledo in 1932. A comparison by Sir Edward Denison

Ross (diplomat, museum curator, university lecturer in Persian, 1871–1940) illustrates the complexity of the relationships between even the fuller manuscripts. He noted that the Toledo manuscript contains two hundred passages that are not found in the Bibliothèque Nationale manuscript, but some three-fifths of these do occur in Ramusio's printed version, and there are some eighty passages which are unique to the Toledo manuscript. One of these is the long description of Russia, a country that no one supposes that Marco Polo visited. Denison Ross, without questioning the reason for the inclusion of this distant and irrelevant country, simply states that 'no one can fail to be struck by the minuteness and abundance of details, which could not possibly have been invented'.[26]

The best modern versions of the work, such as those by Latham and Moule and Pelliot, include passages from various versions and rely a great deal upon Ramusio and the Toledo manuscript. The reason is simple: many of the 'best' passages do seem to occur only in the late versions of Ramusio and Toledo (fifteenth century). These include, for example, the 'crypto-Christians' or Manichaeans of Fuzhou, who are found only in the Toledo manuscript, and Ramusio's long description of Hangzhou.[27] The complications of creating an interesting version are easily seen in Moule and Pelliot's translation, where the confusing variety of manuscripts used to create a coherent and interesting text involves up to forty-two references to different versions per page.

In order to try to decide how many writers were involved in the compilation of the text, various versions of the *Description of the World* were subjected to computer analysis.[28] This demonstrated the extremely varied use of vocabulary, and led the analyst to the conclusion that a second ghost writer might have taken over at one point. This is difficult to prove definitively for none of the texts analysed are 'original', none in Marco Polo's own hand. Given the lapse of time and the fast-expanding medieval development of knowledge about the East, we can only conclude that surviving versions include interpolations by others into some base text which, as Benedetto has demonstrated, is long lost and known only through copies of copies.

Fine editions of the *Description of the World* include illustrations from fourteenth-century manuscripts which depict the Polos, the Khan and many of the places described. Perhaps the most beautiful illustrations are to be found in the 'best text' in the Bibliothèque Nationale, once owned by the Duc de Berry,[29] and the late fourteenth-century manuscript in the Bodleian Library, Oxford, which is a compilation, also including accounts of missionary travels such as that of Odoric of Pordenone and a tale of Alexander the Great. The illustrations, though charming, are deceptive, for they date from a hundred or more years after the events. They are exceptionally attractive and, particularly in their depictions of fabulous beasts like the roc, gryphon and unicorn (or Sumatran rhinoceros transmogrified?), tell us more about the late medieval imagination and belief in fabulous beasts and lands of headless men than what the Polos might actually have looked like.[30]

The language
of the text

Ramusio aside, most agree that the language of the original, lost manuscript of the *Description of the World* must have been a medieval form of French, 'very old and rude French' as Murray has it,[1] as this was the language that would have come most naturally to the ghost-writer Rustichello. However, Ramusio insisted that it was Latin, and others still have suggested that it must have been in the Tuscan dialect.[2] As early as 1827, the Italian scholar Baldelli Boni compared the earliest surviving French and Italian manuscripts and demonstrated the corrupt nature of the second, Italian, group. The translation from French or Romance into Italian dialects led to some mistakes which must have made little sense in places: a description of the '*tres noble cite*' (most noble city) of Xiangyang was turned into the '*delle tre nobile citta*' (three cities), '*bue*' or 'mud' was turned into 'bulls', and '*feels*' (faithful attendants) were made into the '*filz*' (sons.)[3]

At the time that Rustichello was writing, French as we know it had not fully developed. Looking at the surviving early manuscripts, the language is, perhaps, best described as 'Franco-Italian', as it is somewhere between the two. Early translators had difficulties with it, perhaps because Rustichello's use of language was apparently unorthodox. A very serious study of Rustichello's usage notes the 'Italianisation' of the vocal finals and considerable 'ambiguities'. Lists of the verbal forms found illustrate the extreme freedom with which the language was treated. The verb 'to cook' occurs in the following forms, including the infinitive and various past tenses: *cuocere, cucire, cuet, cuittes* and *cot* (half-way between cooked and hot?). One expert has put many passages of various versions of the text to computer analysis and, rather than concluding that it was necessarily Rustichello being inconsistent, suggested the work may have been written by a series of ghost writers, each bringing his own favourite verbal endings to the task.[4] If the method of compilation described in the Prologue is accepted, a stream of collaborators is difficult to imagine, stretching the terms even of 'house arrest', and work on the development of the Romance languages does suggest considerable fluidity. In any case, as the 'original' manuscript does not survive, and surviving versions appear to have been added to in many cases, variant language use is very difficult to follow consistently. Nevertheless, despite its inconsistencies of verbal forms and endings, the language is quite easy to read and great fun, and quite a lot easier to understand than Esperanto.

An enormous amount of work on the language of the texts was done by Paul Pelliot (1878–1945), one of the most famous French sinologists, who, early in his career, had trekked across Central Asia like the Polos, though he was searching for documents and artefacts of the lost civilisations that had flourished in the area some hundreds of years before the rise of the Mongols in the twelfth century.[5]

Pelliot worked with an Englishman, A. C. Moule, on a new translation of the *Description of the World,* which was inspired by the recent discovery of the early fifteenth-century Latin version, the 'Toledo manuscript', with its exciting new contents. Pelliot's contribution to the joint effort was two volumes of notes on the names of places and people found in the various manuscripts and printed editions. He discovered enormous variations in spellings, which led to equally enormous confusion, but his most interesting conclusion was that the majority of the names used in the texts, however they were spelled, were based on Persian words.[6]

His notes are arranged alphabetically and prefaced by the ten to twenty variants found in different manuscript editions. Thus '*facfur*', which he describes as a 'correct transcription of Persian ... a common designation of the Chinese Emperor in Mussulman sources', is listed as appearing as *facfur* in French (or Franco-Italian as Moule calls it), as *alefur* or *fatfur* in some Venetian versions, as *fanfur* in Ramusio, as *scafogi* in a Venetian version preserved in Lucca, and as *synifey* in a German version written by a distracted copyist.

These wild variants demonstrate the problems of manuscript transmission, for careless copying can decisively alter meaning or create utter confusion. The bizarre transmission of proper names was perhaps not a huge problem for fifteenth-century readers, as these strange names were exotically meaningless whether transcribed well or badly, but as the Luccan version has both *scafogi* and *fuschur,* its readers must have been left with the impression that the Chinese Son of Heaven had many exotic and incomprehensible names.

The widespread use of Persian, Arabic or Turkish proper names is one of the first major puzzles of Marco Polo's book. This is apparent in the use, for example, of a Persian term to designate the Emperor of China where you might expect Marco Polo to have used a Mongol or Chinese term acquired during his seventeen years at the court in Peking.

However, it is possible that one reason for his omission of Chinese and Mongol lay in the medieval use of various *lingua franca,* for the practicalities of contact with foreigners dictated the use of 'common' languages in medieval times, just as they do today. It may please the French (who, in the face of excessive anglicisation of their language, have just passed legislation insisting that French must be the language of all French conferences) to know that in the medieval period French was, in effect, a *lingua franca* of much of Europe and used by European pilgrims and crusaders in the Holy Land. It appears that Persian and Turkish were similarly used further east, as far as the Mongol heartlands, for Persian- and Turkish-speaking traders and monks dominated the trade routes across Central Asia.[7]

Most writers on Marco Polo agree that the dominant language of proper names is Persian. Leonardo Olschki notes, too, that Persian was the language used by foreigners in the service of the Mongols though it did not have the official status of Turkish Uighur.[8] It is also generally agreed that Marco Polo might have known Persian, which, in a family that traded from the Crimea and beyond, would have been a useful, not to say necessary, skill. Thus the use of Persian terms is not necessarily surprising. In one text, Marco Polo mentions being shown round Fuzhou by a 'wise saracen'.[9] It must be presumed that they conversed in Persian and, though it is an isolated reference to interpreters and guides, it raises the question of how travellers made their way across Central Asia and who they took with them.

The problem of interpretation was raised by John of Plano Carpini, who was sent by Pope Innocent IV in 1246 to the court of the Mongol Khan Güyüg (grandson of Qinghis).[10] Pope Innocent's letter, written in Latin and translated into Mongolian for Güyüg by his court scribes, expressed concern at the Mongols' slaughter of Hungarians and other Christians and enjoined the Mongol Khan to embrace Christianity and be baptised.

Güyüg's response was drafted in Mongolian and he apparently asked whether the Pope had anyone who could read Mongolian, Persian or Russian. Friar John explained that the languages were not current and asked that the court scribes explain the draft to him so that he could translate it into Latin there and then. The Latin version is recorded and a Persian version survives in the Vatican archives. The content of the draft was not what the Pope might have hoped for. Rather than accept papal supremacy, Güyüg demanded that the Pope pay homage to the Mongols and come to his court to accept Mongol commands. He suggested that the death of Hungarians was the 'will of God',[11] as was Mongol supremacy, and he further questioned the Pope's assertion that he represented the only true Christianity. Güyüg's family and court favoured Nestorian Christians, who may well have acted as linguists in the chain of interpretation between Latin and Mongolian as they, being mainly of Near Eastern origin, must have been familiar with both.

Poor William of Rubruck (who was in Mongolia from 1253 to 1255) suffered from an interpreter who was so frequently drunk that Rubruck could not tell whether his opinions were correctly transmitted to the Khan.[12]

It is possible that the Polos travelled with Nestorian interpreters or other Persian traders and this could account for the dominance of Persian or Turkish vocabulary. Pelliot discusses quite a lot of the nouns referring to objects which are translated into an existing European term, though these themselves often represent an early borrowing from the Persian, reflecting the language of the traders who first brought the objects to Western Europe. *Calamanz* (cuttlefish or ink horn) was 'Latin or Persian'; *azuro, azurro* or *acur* are used for lapis lazuli and are identifiable and acceptable renderings for the colour of the material; *ambra* or *ambrum* are used for ambergris and closely resemble the terms still used in French and Italian; camphorwood is described as *canfur* or *fansur,* based on a borrowing from Arabic current at the time, although the *fansur* version may be a confusion with the place of origin (on Sumatra). Similarly, *cremosi* (*carmosi, charmexini*) is glossed as French *cramoisie* and

English crimson, a colour term long borrowed from the Turkish (possibly Arabic) and widely used to refer to a deep purple cloth.

One of the most fascinating terms used in the text is porcelain (*porcelaine, porcelane, porcellana, porzelane, porcelliane*). Polo's uses reflect the then-current confusion between cowrie shells, which were used in Africa and ancient China as a form of coinage (their use persisting in Yunnan into the thirteenth century), and the Chinese ceramic still known as porcelain; both of which, in Europe, were referred to by the same term, which, confusingly, also covered mother-of-pearl vessels and the plant, purslane. Marco Polo himself uses the same word to mean both cowrie shells and porcelain. The term provokes nearly eight pages of closely packed argument by Pelliot,[13] who discusses the use of the term 'porcelain' to refer to cowrie shells as a reference to their resemblance either to a pig's back (Latin *porcus* – pig) or the female genitalia (French *pucelage* – maidenhood). Cowries appear to have been imported to Western Europe before the *Description of the World* was written since they are listed in the *Consolat del mar* (Barcelona, *c.* 1250) and the use of the term porcelain for China-ware (ceramics) is noted in the context of a description of the ware by the Arab traveller Suleiman (ninth century). The confusion of terms may have given rise to a long-held European belief that the mysteriously fine, translucent and resonant ceramics were made from crushed shells, though they were, in fact, made from a special clay, a fact which was not brought to European attention until 1712, in a report by the Jesuit Père D'Entre-colles.[14] Further confusing us over the origin of the term, Pelliot quotes a wonderful description, almost contemporary with Polo, in the *Libellus de notitia orbis* (1402), which states that the material, porcelain, was known in Latin as *porcellanum* (purslane) because greenish-grey porcelain vessels of the type now known as celadon were the same colour as the herb.[15]

Another term which sends Professor Pelliot into pages of complex linguistic reconstruction is '*camlet*' (*cambelloti, chamelles, gianbellotti, zambelotti* etc), a kind of cloth. Dr Johnson's dictionary defines 'Camelot' as 'silk or camel's hair; also all silk or velvet, especially pily or plushy'. Pelliot inclines to the camel-hair aspect and notes that John of Marignolli (papal envoy to the Khans of 1330–1440) brought back a cloak of *camalli*, which he said was not unlike that worn by John the Baptist and possibly similar to the clothing he thought Adam and Eve might have worn, although I thought their problems arose from a lack of clothes.

Another puzzling textile term is '*sendal*', which in medieval texts normally indicated silk taffeta (and occurs in Pegolotti's merchants' handbook as *zendado*). In the description of a wrestling match between the gigantic daughter of Qaidu (a descendant of Chagatai, son of Qinghis) and a prospective husband (who would marry her if he won), both are described by Polo and Rustichello as wearing clothes of *sendal*.[16] The context worries Professor Pelliot, who is more at home in a book-lined study than faced with female wrestlers of strapping proportions. He considers the implications of dress during this peculiar method of choosing a husband and ponders the advantages of silk taffeta over leather (which occurs in two manuscript versions): 'Taffeta may not seem to be a very appropriate material for competitors in a wrestling match, but no more or still less is leather, and we must make due allowance for the solemnity of the competition and the quality of the participants . . .'[17] Whether lightly clad in silk or protected by leathers, the princess won two-nil and never married, preferring to accompany her father in battle and reverse the normal male custom of rape and pillage by carrying off knights to her own camp.[18]

Some of the words associated with the Mongols that occur in the text had already been used by writers such as William of Rubruck and John of Plano Carpini. *Kumis,* the fermented mare's milk that the Mongols drank, is varyingly given as *charanis, guemis, chemins* and *chenus,* in variants of the Turkish *qimiz* (Rubruck has *comos*). The Mongol term is *asuk* or *usuk* but the Turkish version had passed early into Persian and Arabic.

Professor Pelliot acknowledges that in many cases, the vocabulary is purely Near Eastern. The sand grouse, *Syrrhaptes pallassii,* a common enough bird in desert regions, known in Chinese as *shaji* (sand fowl), is referred to as a *bagherlac* (a Turkish version). It is easy enough to imagine that Italian travellers, sighting a bird in the desert, might enquire of fellow travellers who knew the region (and were by inference of Near Eastern origin) what the bird was and accept its name as *bagherlac.*

The personal names, especially of Chinese and Mongols mentioned, are of particular interest. Despite the seventeen years spent by Marco in China in the Khan's service, of some sixty or more personal names examined by Pelliot only three appear in a vaguely Chinese form. Most of the others are the names of Mongols and the renderings of these frequently agree with Carpini and Rubruck, as well as the Persian historian, Rashīd al-Dīn (1247–1317). He was an almost exact contemporary of Marco Polo's, although he served with the Western Mongols, and his history of the Mongols appears to have been first written down in 1306–7, over a decade after the creation of the *Description of the World.* Thus similarities between Rashīd and Marco Polo's books, both in terminology and errors, are coincidental, but they seem to suggest that Persian versions of Mongol names were already current.

Of the three apparently Chinese names, two, Li Tan and Wang Zhu, are mentioned in a chapter dealing with China proper. The other, Vonsamcin, is referred to in a passage relating to Japan, which everyone agrees the Polos did not visit.

Li Tan (who appears as Bitan sangon, Liyacin, Liitam sangon, Lucansor and Lufa) was the son of Li Quan (d.

1231), a horse-trader who had fought for the Chinese Song government and was rewarded with an official position in 1218. He used his position to build up a personal power base, but in 1227 he capitulated to the Mongols on their invasion of Northern China and was rewarded with another position in Shandong province. He died in Yangzhou in 1231 during an attack by the Southern Song army. His son (some say adopted son), Li Tan, succeeded him in Shandong, where, in 1262, he raised an army of his own, but was encircled in Jinan (the capital of Shandong) by Shi Tianze and killed.[19] Polo's account, which occurs in a wide spread of manuscripts, gets the date wrong by ten years (1272), gets the place wrong by stating that it was Dongpingfu, and further confuses the issue by stating that Li Tan was executed together with one Nangiatai.

The question of Nangiatai is, as Professor Pelliot notes, 'a difficult one'.[20] There are about ten Nangiadai (a more correct Mongol form) listed in the *Yuan shi* (*History of the Yuan Dynasty*, the official history compiled by the succeeding Ming dynasty on the basis of official archives), one of whom is credited with distinguishing himself in the capture and execution of Li Tan, rather than being executed with him. A further complication of the Nangiatai/Nangiadai question is whether Polo actually meant Mongatai (of whom twenty appear in the *Yuan shi*). If he did mean Mongatai, then Professor Pelliot, his knickers already twisted, notes that the most likely Mongatai was apparently unconnected with the campaign against Li Tan. However, Professor Pelliot thinks that the confusion may have arisen from the fact that, though the Yan family held Dongpingfu (just north of Jinan in Shandong province) at the time, Mongatai's grandfather, who had been officially appointed 'resident' (and was later succeeded by Mongatai's uncle), was theoretically more important than the Yan family in Dongpingfu, and that this may have caused some of Marco Polo's confusion. Or not.

Wang Zhu (Vanchu) occurs only in Ramusio. His name is

somewhat mysterious. He is credited, together with another Chinese, with killing Ahmad (Acmat), Qubilai's most powerful minister, in 1282. Here, again, the confusions of names, people and events are almost impossible to untangle, particularly since the Chinese sources suggest that Rashīd al-Dīn got as deeply confused as Marco Polo. It is known that Ahmad was a native of Banakath, near Tashkent, and his biography is included in the *Yuan shi*. In all sources he is described as resorting to black magic in order to get his way with Qubilai, and Marco Polo also elaborates upon his habit of seizing pretty women. He seems to have been able to have his way for some twenty years, effectively ruling Peking, until two 'Cathayans' (Chinese) decided to get rid of him when Qubilai was out of town. Their uprising involved much killing of people with beards (Mongols, Saracens and Christians, but not the clean-shaven Chinese) before they managed to behead Ahmad by tricking him into kneeling before what he thought was the son of Qubilai. The two Cathayans are called Cenchu (also only occurring in Ramusio) and Vanchu. According to Polo, Cenchu's mother, daughter and wife had all been ravished by Ahmad,[21] and he had 1,000 men with him. Since is it not easy to reconcile Cenchu with any known Chinese person, Pelliot assumes that the term is not a name but rather a designation, *qian hu* (Chinese for 1,000 persons or households) or *chiliarch*, one in charge of 1,000 soldiers.

Vanchu, the other conspirator, is described by Moule as a *myriarch* (in charge of 10,000 soldiers) with the 'name' Vanchu being a version of *wan hu* (Chinese for 10,000 persons). A minor complication (given the general confusion) is that Wang Zhu, if it was indeed he, was, according to Chinese records, not a *myriarch* but a *chiliarch* (able to muster 1,000 rather than 10,000 men). If we take Vanchu as his personal name, then Wang Zhu is known to have taken part in the conspiracy to kill Ahmad, thus Ramusio's version is vindicated as far as content is concerned (though marked down for spelling and arithmetic).

Unfortunately, the story does not end here. Wang Zhu and the *chiliarch* were both executed by a guard at the palace who interrupted their assassination. Rashīd al-Dīn calls him Turgan or Targan whilst Ramusio's version of the Polo text has Cogatai, a Mongol name that Professor Pelliot reluctantly concludes is 'misapplied'.[22] He thinks that the person mentioned must have been Gao Xi (known to have been present and recorded in the *Yuan shi*). Pelliot rejects the suggestion that Cogatai is a phonetic rendering of Gao Xi and regrets the fact that Gao Xi had a perfectly good Mongol name of his own, Sira, conferred by Qubilai. Other candidates known from Chinese sources to have been present are the Mongol Bodun, who is unlikely to have had an alias, and Jiang Jiusi, who was pure Chinese with no Mongol name.

The third 'Chinese' personal name to occur is Vonsamcin (which occurs in a range of manuscripts as Ionsamcaym, Nonsan, Samin, Vosanhim, Vansancon, and Vori). Pelliot glosses it as that of Fan Wenhu (d. 1301), a military leader who went over to the Mongols and, at Qubilai's order, led an expedition against Japan in 1281 which was beaten back by a typhoon. The distance between Fan Wenhu and Vonsamcin is explained as a combination term, using Fan's surname and one of his titles, *canzheng* (State Counsellor). Polo describes the disastrous outcome of the expedition most vividly, although he rather ruins the effect by, once again, getting the other name wrong. He says that Counsellor Fan was accompanied by 'Abakan'.[23] Pelliot translates this as Alaqan (1233–81) but notes that Alaqan was too ill to take part in the expedition for which he had been nominated and his place may have been taken by one Atahai. Pelliot concludes his entry on Abacan with the benefit of the doubt: 'As usual, Polo, accurate as to the main events

and names, is wrong when he comes to the specific part
played by each individual.'

Of the three references to Chinese people by Chinese
names, only one could possibly have been known to the
Polos, had they been in Peking at the time of the assassination of Ahmad (1282). Given the absence of dates and the
descriptions of trips to Yunnan and Burma and the South,
it is impossible to tell whether they were in the capital at
the time. Li Tan's uprising and death occurred before the
Polos claimed to have reached China, and since all authorities agree that the Polos never went to Japan, Counsellor
Fan's unsuccessful expedition could only have been known
through hearsay or accounts written by others.

The names of places in the *Description of the World* present
complications both of translation and location. The scope of
the work, which opens with the sentence 'Let me begin
with Armenia' (varyingly translated as 'And first about Her-
menia the Less')[24] and covers everywhere from Constantinople to Sumatra by way of India and Central Asia, requires
an enormous number of place names. Many of these are
rendered in ways that would have been familiar to the more
sophisticated or widely-travelled of Marco Polo's contemporaries. Professor Pelliot compared his versions with 'those
occurring on contemporary maps and those used by
contemporary travellers. Many are still recognisable: Baudac
(Baghdad), Cascar (Kashgar), Babilonie (though Polo
meant Egypt), Bangala (Bengal according to Pelliot, though
others disagree), Trepesonde (Trabzon), Mogedaxo
(probably Mogadishu) and Java. Some names were better
known because of the Crusades (Jerusalem and Acre) and,
owing to the pre-eminence of Arab travellers, many names
derive from the Arabic, such as Angaman (Andaman),
Basora (Basra) and Cotan (Khotan).

Names that were less well known include those of Chinese
places. Some of these baffle Pelliot and in many cases, he
noted that the version used was 'known among Persian-

speaking circles'. Thus where forms represent attempts to romanise Chinese names, they are rarely unique to Polo and usually represent Persian attempts to pronounce Chinese names. Examples of this type include Chemeinfu for Kaipingfu, Pianfu for Pingyangfu, Quengianfu for Xi'anfu and Taianfu for Tiayuanfu. A large number of these names occur in a similar form in Rashīd al-Dīn, bearing out Pelliot's theory that forms were based on those current among Persian speakers. Names appearing in a very similar form in Rashīd al-Dīn include Tundinfu for Dongpingfu, Yangiu for Yanzhou and Giogiu for Zhuozhou, and there are several examples that occur in both Rashīd al-Dīn and the account given by Odoric of Pordenone, such as Fugiu for Fuzhou, Singui matu for Xinzhou matou or Xinzhou harbour, and Taidu for Dadu. Some concur with Rashīd and versions given by William of Rubruck such as Cauli for Korea (probably based on the old Chinese name for Korea, Gaoli).

China itself was referred to by several names. Polo used Catai (Achate, Alochayray, Anchases, Atan, Chattau and *la ducata* in various manuscripts), or Cathay, to refer to northern China, as did many of his contemporaries. The name is thought to derive from Khitan, an Altaic tribe that founded the Liao dynasty and ruled northern China from 907 to 1125. Southern China was often referred to, by Polo as well as Rashīd and other travellers, as Mangi or Manzi, often (incorrectly) assumed to derive from a Chinese term, *manyi*, which meant 'southern barbarians'. Polo also referred to China as Cin (Chuigi, Cino, Zino, Ciri), one of the two names by which China was known in Europe, which is thought to derive from a very old Indian name for China based upon the Qin dynasty (221–206 BC), the other being Seres, referring to silk.

Polo's use of Cambaluc, based on the Turkish term for a royal city (*han-baliq*), for Peking was quite normal, for the same name appears in Rashīd al-Dīn, John of Montecorvino (1291–93) and Odoric of Pordenone (1320s), and it was apparently the common Central Asian term for Peking at the time. Peking (a sixteenth century Jesuit rendering of Beijing or 'northern capital') has been known by many names throughout its history, from Yanjing (Swallow capital) to Zhongdu (Middle capital) and Nanjing (Southern capital), though at the time of the Polos it was known to the Chinese as Dadu (Great capital).

One of the sights of Peking today is the long stone bridge at Wanping, known to foreigners as the Marco Polo bridge and to the Chinese (today) as Lugouqiao or Lugou bridge. Polo's name for it is Pulisanghin, translated by Pelliot as either 'Stone bridge' in Persian or 'Bridge of the Sanggan' in Sino-Persian (Sanggan being a name for the river at the time), and Pelliot considered the term to be strongly Persian in origin.

A number of places are wrongly sited: Cacionfu is linked by Pelliot to Hezhongfu, but Polo has it on the wrong side of the Yellow river: Caiciu might be Jiezhou or Jiangzhou, but is in the wrong place in both cases; Vuguen is identified by Pelliot as Yanping, but the distances and times do not fit, either; and Vugiu (Wuzhou) is more happily situated as Lanji, though the names do not fit well.

Polo was not the only writer to get the places wrong. Rashīd al-Dīn's accounts of places like the south-western province of Yunnan were equally inaccurate and, interestingly, appear to repeat Polo's errors. Polo's use of Persian terms might suggest he could have been working from Persian sources. However, we know Rashīd al-Dīn was writing, not a travelogue, but an account of the Mongol empire, which was firmly based on secondary sources. Just as their accounts of the Wang Zhu episode resemble each other but differ from the Chinese sources, their references to Gaindu, somewhere in Yunnan, are equally difficult to pin down. So are references to Iaci (Polo) and Yaci (Rashīd), which they both say is near Yunnanfu. Pelliot, failing to find anything remotely resembling the name, suggests that it may be a reference to the capital of the adjoining kingdom of Dali, which lies beside the huge Er hai ('Ear sea', from its shape). The Er hai was apparently known by the Mongols as 'Duck lake', which Pelliot translates into Chinese as *yachi*, or 'duck pond'. The size of the Er hai, enough of a sea, lengthways at least, for the far shore to be invisibly distant, makes Duck Pond an improbable name, and it might be better just to regard this as another problem insoluble at this distance, a Chinese whisper translated from Persian.

8

Omissions
and inclusions

Marco Polo's apparent failure to pick up even a few Chinese or Mongol place-names in his seventeen-year stay in China remains puzzling. His apparent curiosity about the places and things he saw obviously did not extend to the languages by which he was surrounded.

Pelliot's complex work on the language raised many doubts as to Marco Polo's accuracy as well as the foundation for his information, but Professor Pelliot, though frequently baffled, always left Marco Polo with the benefit of the doubt. However, the German Mongolist Herbert Franke queried Marco Polo's veracity partly on the grounds of the contents of his book, most notably things that he omitted from his description of China.[1]

In the popular imagination, Marco Polo's descriptive gifts provided much significant information on the inventions and exotica of the East. In his descriptions of rare and costly luxury goods from the Near and Far East, Marco Polo's eye was that of a merchant accustomed to dealing in such commodities rather than a papal observer; for one thing he was interested in the value of money, which the missionary William of Rubruck did not mention. Some of the things Marco Polo described were just beginning to be known in Europe, such as porcelain, and it is worth looking at the things he included, as well as his omissions, for they help to create an idea of the acquisitive audience for whom he was writing.

His description of porcelain, though linguistically confusing, must have been of great contemporary significance. At a time when Europeans were using heavy, solid, but easily chipped earthenware vessels, the few examples of porcelain that made their way across the Asian land mass must have seemed of a mysterious lightness, elegance and strength. Porcelain is made from a very fine clay, fired to a high temperature. It is characterised by the fusion of the body and the glaze, a resonant note when struck and, when the body is fine enough, translucence, all characteristics lacking in the more robust earthenwares and stonewares of Marco Polo's Europe. It was all the more fascinating because the method of manufacture was quite unknown (it took European potters some 500 years of unsuccessful experiments, mistakenly using crushed shells and bones, to discover the secret).[2]

Fine white porcelain was exported from China in enormous quantities by the Arabs from the time of the Tang dynasty (618–907), for the durable and elegant white wares were superior to anything produced anywhere else in the world at the time. Such isolated examples as made their way to thirteenth-century Europe were almost certainly bought from Arab middlemen.

Marco Polo's description of porcelain appears to locate its origin in the province of Fujian. Immediately, the sort of problems that dogged Professor Pelliot arise, for Marco sited its production at the mysteriously named town of Tingiu (or Linigui, Tranguay, Tyunguy, Tinguise in various manuscript editions). He described the preparation of the clay[3] and said that the ware was 'azure' and 'glassy'. The difficulty of locating the kiln source is compounded by the colour reference. Pelliot takes '*accuri*' or azure to mean green and identifies the ware as a green celadon of the type produced widely in southern China at the time. This identification makes it more difficult to identify the town where it was produced since none of the celadon centres had names closely resembling Tingiu (or Tranguay or Linigui).

One of the earliest recorded pieces of Chinese porcelain to reach Europe was a *qingbai* vase, now known as the Fonthill vase. This arrived at almost the same time as Marco Polo's return, in about 1300, was later fitted with silver mounts at the order of Louis the Great of Hungary (1348–82), and eventually acquired by the National Museum of Ireland in the mid nineteenth century.[4] It is possible that the Fonthill vase provides a clue to Marco Polo's siting of porcelain manufacture, for *qingbai* ware, a white ware produced at many southern Chinese kilns, has a glassy glaze that is often greeny-blue, which you might possibly describe as '*accuri*' or azure, where it collects in the base of bowls or in drips. *Qingbai* fragments of the Song (960–1279) and Mongol Yuan (1279–1368) period have been found in the Dehua kiln sites,[5] antedating the production of creamy white *blanc de chine*. A possible candidate for the site, stretching transliteration, might be Tongan, also in Fujian, which produced green wares and *qingbai* during the Song and Yuan periods[6] and seems to have specialised in export wares, as noted by Polo.

Another example of relevance is the so-called 'Marco Polo jar' in the Treasury of St Mark's in Venice.[7] The white jar is lobed and covered with a moulded floral decoration and a shining glaze. It is considered to date from the thirteenth or fourteenth century, though there is nothing but tradition to link it with Marco Polo, and it certainly does not accord with the account of his return with only the clothes he stood up in. Interestingly, it is an early example of *blanc de chine*, a white ware with a thicker body and a creamy appearance (without the green glassy drips seen on *qingbai* wares) made at kilns in Dehua in Fujian, but not in

Tongan. Thus it does not fit with either the green wares or, by stretching the azure, *qingbai*, possibly described by Polo.

Though luxury goods dominate Marco Polo's descriptions of foreign produce, he did include some more domestic peculiarities such as the use of coal. Coal had been used as a fuel in China for 2000 years before Marco Polo described it and, though it had apparently been known in Bronze Age Wales, it was not until the fourteenth or fifteenth century that it was used in England. It was probably unknown to the Italians of the time. It is described in the *Description of the World* quite accurately as 'a kind of large black stones which are dug up from mountains as veins which burn like logs and burn away like charcoal'.[8] It is worth noting that the description appears to be marginally better than that of the slightly later Arab traveller Ibn Baṭṭūṭa (1304–77/8), who described coal as having the colour and consistency of clay (and wrongly stated that the same stuff was used to make porcelain) but also used the comparison with charcoal.[9]

One of the great innovations of Song (960–1279) and Yuan (1279–1368) China was the use of paper money. It was not only the practice of using a substitute for coins, whose worth was based on the actual value of the metal, but the material itself that was unusual, for paper had only just begun to be known in Europe when Marco Polo was writing. Paper had been invented in China sometime during the early Han dynasty (206 BC–AD 220) and its use was widespread by the Tang (618–907) for official documents and printed books, as well as domestically for letters and notes. Arabs had learnt how to make paper from the Chinese, probably in the ninth century, and introduced it to Europe, where it was first manufactured in Spain in the early twelfth century. It was known in early thirteenth-century Italy, though its use for official documents was prohibited in 1221 as it was thought to be too fragile to be durable. The earliest paper mill in Italy was established in Fabriano between 1268 and 1279; thus, at the time that Marco Polo was in China, it must still have been a rare commodity.[10] Since paper was suspect as a material in Europe, it must have been particularly striking to find it used as currency.

Printed promissory notes or drafts (known as 'flying money') were first used by merchants and government agencies in ninth-century China. The system relied upon the well-established trade guilds of merchants, who travelled throughout the country staying at special guild halls built in every major town for merchants from each province. The guild hall for travelling merchants from the distant southern province of Guangdong still stands in Tianjin, its richly carved decoration demonstrating the wealth of the merchant guilds. For the convenience of merchants travelling long distances, paper 'promissory notes' could be used instead of the heavy bronze coinage or great gold and silver boat-shaped ingots normally used in financial transactions. True 'paper money', rather than these promissory notes, appeared in the early eleventh century. During the Mongol era, several issues of paper money were made, printed on small sheets of darkish paper, using a woodblock carved with the Chinese text in reverse, and finally authorised with a red seal in the Mongol script.

In the *Description of the World*, paper money is described in detail as to its convertibility and relative worth.[11] The method of making paper is also described, but the complexities of woodblock-printing (over one hundred years before Gutenberg) are not explored and the notes are only described as 'stamped'. The reference to 'stamping' could arise from the stamped authorisation seal or, perhaps, refer to the whole woodblock itself. (William of Rubruck also described the paper money he saw in Mongolia some thirty years before Marco Polo: 'The everyday currency of Cataia is of paper, the breadth and length of a palm, on which lines are stamped as on Mangu's seal . . .'[12] He did not go into the detail of the exchange rates at all, perhaps because he was not a merchant.

When comparing other accounts of the Mongols and Chinese written by contemporary or near contemporary European visitors, there are some very significant omissions in Polo's text. The very next line in Rubruck's account of paper money (which he only saw in Mongolia as he did not get to China) continues with a description of Chinese writing, which remains one of the most exotically different things about the country, but which does not seem to have struck Marco Polo.

William of Rubruck's extremely brief introduction to the Chinese writing system was inspired by the Chinese characters printed on the bank notes. 'They write with a brush of the sort painters use, and in a single character make several letters that comprise one word.'[13] This is quite a good, if excessively succinct, description of the Chinese writing system, which has no alphabet but up to 40,000 separate characters which represent words. Developed from pictographs and ideographs and a complex system of phonetic loans, characters consist of anything from one to over twenty strokes and were, as William of Rubruck noted, traditionally written with a brush.

The lack of reference to this extraordinarily different script in the *Description of the World* was defended by Leonardo Olschki, who felt that the language was quite inaccessible to Marco Polo as 'a foreigner lacking in any literary or spiritual initiative . . .'.[14] Even if it was incomprehensible, it must have been difficult to miss, for the Mongols themselves were cowed by the Chinese written language. They had only adopted their own writing system in the early thirteenth century[15] and, as nomads, had hardly developed a paper-consuming bureaucracy. In 1279, however, faced with the task of controlling the whole of China, of collecting taxes and administering the law, they had to adopt the Chinese attitude to paper and record-keeping. It has been estimated that the annual tax assessments of one single ministry (the Board of Revenue) required half a million sheets of paper per year during the Tang dynasty (618–907),[16] and the Mongols were compelled to join the paper mountain. They probably added to it, for documents were written in the Mongol script and then translated into Chinese (this in itself presented a problem, for Chinese were not usually allowed to learn Mongol).[17] Though Qubilai is not thought to have been comfortable with classical written Chinese, his successors became increasingly sinicised and adept at Chinese calligraphy and composition.[18]

It is also the case that the Chinese have always used the written language far more widely and with greater inventiveness than we do. Inscriptions praising the natural beauty of a scene were frequently carved into mountain-side cliffs and in the gardens of Suzhou, and on rocks surrounding the lake at Hangzhou, poetic inscriptions by emperors and famous calligraphers were carved into stone. It is not only nature that was embellished and given greater significance by the addition of the beautifully written word: the poetic names of pavilions and temple halls were inscribed on boards over their doors, enhancing the elegant architecture with calligraphy and adding a depth of meaning to scenes or groups of buildings. Thus, even as a traveller unconcerned with the business of government, it would have been difficult to ignore the Chinese script. It is hard to conceive that in the country where paper was invented and the written word revered more than almost anywhere else, a person, even a foreigner, could claim to have served in the government bureaucracy and either fail to notice the Mongol and the Chinese writing systems or consider them of little interest.

Though the *Description of the World* contains references to the use of paper effigies of people, caparisoned horses and camels, and paper money burnt at funerals,[19] the widespread use of woodblock printing (at the time still unknown in Europe) is not mentioned. The markets of the towns that Marco Polo describes would have been full of small book stalls selling cheaply printed popular handbooks and works of fiction, many of which were illustrated. The southern coastal province of Fujian (described by Marco Polo at some length) was a centre of book production during the Song dynasty and known for the export of printed books throughout the country. In Hangzhou (Polo's Kinsai), capital of the Southern Song, one of the seventeen markets was a book market and booksellers clustered around the Orange Garden Pavilion.[20] Despite this, although Marco Polo described the markets, he only described food and silks on sale.

Perhaps even more surprisingly, despite a considerable interest in the edible produce displayed in Hangzhou's markets and the drinks and wines served at imperial banquets, Marco Polo never mentioned tea. Made from the leaves of a southern Chinese bush related to the camellia, tea was drunk in southern China from the Han dynasty (206 BC–AD 220) onwards but, according to written sources including the official history of the Tang and Lu Yu's *Cha jing* (*Classic of Tea*), it only really became widely popular in north China in the late eighth century. From then on it became the standard drink throughout China. Many of the places described in the *Description of the World* are famous for different sorts of tea, like the Wulong of Fujian and the green Longjing of the Hangzhou area, which was prepared with local spring water. Beauty spots that Marco Polo visited, like Hangzhou and Suzhou, were filled with tea-houses of all grades, with simple ones near the meat market and more elegant versions in the better shopping areas. A 1275 description of Hangzhou, written at about the time Marco Polo probably stayed there, described the lacquer trays, porcelain cups, varieties of tea (from plum flower to medicinal brews), and the displays of painting and calligraphy and flowers and bonsai that decorated the tea-houses.[21] Had the Polos been as well-connected as Marco suggests, they would almost certainly have been entertained in such tea-houses, for the Chinese did not entertain at home. Entertaining aside, the street-side tea-houses would have been difficult to miss. Polo describes various varieties of wine, made from grapes, rice and sugar-cane, and it might be argued that, despite the enthusiasm for tea amongst the Arabs and Persians, who had acquired the taste from China, an infusion of boiled leaves would be of no interest to his European audience. It is, however, difficult to imagine a sojourn of seventeen years in China without noticing the popularity of the drink.

However, even if it can be argued that the ghost-writer Rusticello threw out boiled leaves as incredible or lacking in interest, it is difficult to imagine a romance writer discarding a reference to exotic femininity and the peculiar custom of foot-binding.

Yet there are relatively few references to women in the *Description of the World* and nowhere is the practice of foot-binding even mentioned. Marco Polo describes the women of Fujian as very beautiful and the merchants' wives of Hangzhou as decked in silks and jewellery.[22] In a passage occurring only in Ramusio, there is a description of the courtesans of Hangzhou[23] and their seductive techniques, but still no mention of their presumably bound feet.

Foot-binding became popular amongst the upper classes during the Song dynasty (960–1279) when small girls had their toes bent under the soles of their feet and tied with wet bandages (which would shrink as they dried) to create a small, pointed foot.[24] Once the foot had been successfully deformed they were unable to walk far and could never even stand without their foot-bindings, for the bandages formed a necessary support for the hoof-like foot. Eventually, the practice spread until by the early twentieth century it had become virtually universal amongst all but the poorest peasants, who needed able-bodied women to work in the fields. However, the Manchus, who ruled China from 1644 until 1911, never adopted it and neither did the Mongols. Thus it could be argued that during the Mongol period, when the Polos were supposed to have been in China, it was not so widespread and, since women whose feet had been bound could not move far, possibly invisible to foreign travellers.

It could also be argued that the enclosure of women meant that Marco Polo would have seen few upper-class Chinese women. It is perhaps significant that he describes merchants' wives, for merchants were traditionally despised and their sons barred from entry into the bureaucratic class (unless they changed their status to that of landowner by investing their wealth in the purchase of land). Thus merchants' wives were perhaps not immediately affected by the upper-class fashion for foot-binding and were maybe more likely to flaunt their wealth on the streets, where they could be seen by strangers.

In later traditional China, it was rare for a foreigner or outsider to see respectable women other than servants. Despite Confucius' (*c.* 500 BC) early advocation of the separation of men and women (to the point where it was considered improper for a man to reach out a hand to save his sister-in-law from drowning), the strict enclosure of women does not seem to have been widespread until the Ming (1368–1644). A famous painting depicting the capital city of Kaifeng in the early Song period (*c.* 1100–1130) shows only a few women in the streets of the city,[25] but there are at least a few. By the Ming, enclosure had become much stricter, with upper-class women confined to the side and rear courtyards of the family home and not introduced to male visitors even within the home. However, it is quite possible that in the laxer days of Mongol rule, Marco Polo might have seen women with unbound feet on the streets of Chinese towns.

Nonetheless, Friar Odoric of Pordenone, who travelled in China from 1320 and dictated his memoirs in 1330, describes foot-binding in South China, in conjunction with the then current male fashion for growing enormously long fingernails.[26] Long fingernails, protected by jewelled nail guards, remained fashionable amongst women until the Qing dynasty (1644–1911), although by that time gentlemen usually only allowed one or two fingernails to grow long, as an indication that they had no need to take part in manual labour. Odoric's whole passage about foot-binding was lifted almost verbatim by Sir John Mandeville, writing in the mid fourteenth century: 'The mark of nobility in women there is to have small feet; and so as soon as they are born, they bind their feet so tightly that they cannot grow as they should.'[27] It does seem inconceivable that fashions could have changed so rapidly within fifty years that Marco Polo did not see bound feet whilst the pious Friar Odoric, who did not have the entrée into society that Marco Polo claimed, described them in some detail.

Aside from women, another activity that Marco Polo either failed to notice or lacked interest in was cormorant fishing. One of the sights for today's travellers on the river from Guilin is the use of tame cormorants by fishermen. Supplied with a ring around their necks so that they cannot swallow large fish, the birds dive from bamboo rafts and bring back their catch. The sight fascinated members of Lord Macartney's embassy to China (1792–94): 'This bird is so like another species of the pelican . . . or common cormorant . . . these birds will seize and grip fast fishes that are not less than their own weight . . .'[28] They were also noticed by Friar Odoric, who left the earliest description to reach Europe of cormorants 'catching large numbers of fish and ever as they caught them putting them of their own accord into the baskets'.[29]

In Marco Polo's favour, it is argued against the German Mongolist that, given the lapse of time before the compilation of the *Description of the World*, he may have forgotten about things. Some things, like tea-drinking, might have been put before Rustichello and discarded as of no interest to the general public or, given the variations of texts and multitude of copyists, erasures may have occurred. He may, equally, have so lacked interest in Chinese culture or been so narrowly European in outlook that the writing system, for example, was of no interest to him, though it is claimed in his Prologue that he mastered Mongol at least and spoke directly to Qubilai Khan. In these arguments, the failure to describe foot-binding seems the most extraordinary for it, almost above all else, certainly fascinated later travellers. Barrow described bound feet seen in 1793–4 during the Macartney embassy[30] and they were illustrated in Staunton's account of the embassy.[31] Early photographers in China took photographs of them and my impression after looking through the collections is that the largest single group of artefacts held in the Chinese collections of the Museum of Mankind in London is the group of tiny embroidered shoes made for bound feet, brought back in their hundreds by nineteenth- and early twentieth-century European visitors and missionaries.

Thus, it is puzzling that tea and bound feet, things that symbolise China in the Western imagination, are missing from an avowedly popular text. Nor does he mention chopsticks . . .

9

Ice-cream and spaghetti

It seems obvious through his lack of reference that Marco Polo did not bring a taste for tea back to thirteenth-century Venice (and it was not until 400 years later that Europe became desperate for tea) but some of the most prevalent popular legends about him concern his possible importation of spaghetti, ravioli and ice-cream from China to Europe. However, the question of Marco Polo's influence on the culinary arts of Italy (or China, depending upon whether you are Chinese or Italian) is not one that can be easily decided by careful reading of his book.

Pepper, pears, dog-meat and all manner of fish are listed in his description of the markets of Hangzhou but he did not, unfortunately, resort to the same detail in describing the food he must have eaten. He mentioned the use of noodles, the consumption of rice and all sorts of meats (including human flesh in Fujian) but never described how things were cooked or served (nor did he mention much in the way of vegetables). He is not alone in this, for the first British travellers to China were equally unobservant or failing in detail. Aeneas Anderson, valet to Lord Macartney on the first British Embassy to China (1792–94), merely noted that 'their manner of dressing meat is by cutting it in very small pieces which they fry in oil, with roots and herbs.

They have plenty of soy and vinegar, which they add by way of sauce,' though he found rice 'a most excellent substitute for bread'.[1] Elsewhere, Anderson refers to meals as 'messes', one hopes in the military sense. Even such scarce detail is lacking in Marco Polo's account, but the mere fact of an Italian visiting China at such an early date has given rise to much speculation about who influenced whom. Nineteenth-century historians, many of whom followed diffusion theories, looked for the inevitable link and fell upon Marco Polo.

The question of influence is complicated by the fact that Italy and China, two countries that take such pride in their culinary heritage, mysteriously enjoy some remarkably similar foods. Pasta in all its Italian varieties is paralleled by Chinese noodles, also appearing in a variety of shapes, though usually tending to be long and thinnish, rather than butterfly or shell-shaped. Thus argument arises over whether Marco Polo took spaghetti and ravioli to China, where they were transformed into *jiaozi* and noodles, staple foods of the north, or whether he brought noodles and *jiaozi* back to Italy, where they became spaghetti and ravioli.

Nineteenth-century diffusionism held that everything had a single origin and, from the Stone Age, inventors travelled the world amazing other civilisations with their discoveries. In pre-war Vienna, anthropology students were taught, 'Cooking with water was invented only once,'[2] as if the inventor travelled the world proudly demonstrating his discovery and personally effecting its transmission from culture to culture. In some cases, the transmission of a technique can be clearly demonstrated, as in the movement of paper manufacture from China through the Arab world to Spain and Italy, but in other cases, diffusionism tends to downplay human ingenuity.

However, it does seem that in this case the similarities between Italian pasta and Chinese noodles may well owe something to the Arab world, which lay conveniently between the two and whose merchants controlled much of the movement of goods between them. Claudia Roden, whose first cookery book was on Middle Eastern food but who has subsequently won two cook-book prizes for work on Italian food,[3] says 'Persians are at the bottom of pasta' and archaeologists exploring China's early food production concur; so Arab influence seems to be responsible both for Chinese noodles and Italian pasta.

Wheat, ground into flour and without the addition of yeast or other raising agents, lends itself to the production of both pasta and noodles. It was the occupation of Sicily in 827 by an Arab army that brought hard durum wheat to Italy. Easy to grow but difficult to mill, it is the main ingredient of pasta. Durum wheat pasta then gradually spread northwards throughout Italy.[4] Just as Persian vocabulary is widely used in the *Description of the World*, the vocabulary of the Arabs in Sicily is commemorated in a type of thin spaghetti still known by the old Arabic name, *itriya*. Curiously, despite the demonstrated introduction and northwards movement, there seems to have been a separate Genoese (not Venetian, alas) tradition of pasta-making, which also owed a great deal to Arab influence. Small lasagne-like squares of pasta are called *mandili di sea* or 'silk handkerchiefs', *mandil* being the Arab word for a handkerchief, and in Genoa, linguini are known as *tria*, another Arabic word.[5]

Noodles and *jiaozi*, the very similar dishes eaten in north China, all also made from durum wheat flour, and are likewise thought to be the result of Arab influence via Central Asia. The durum wheat used for Chinese noodles and *jiaozi* is thought to have originated in Western Asia.[6]

One of the more difficult dishes is Italian ravioli, very similar to Chinese *jiaozi* (usually translated as dumplings but far closer to ravioli than the unstuffed, leavened European dumpling). The earliest surviving *jiaozi* or dumpling, an eighth-century funerary offering of spiced meat in a pasta parcel, was excavated in the Gobi desert,[7] in an area of China which had been dominated by Arab culture at the time; it can still be seen in the Turfan Museum. Unlike noodles, ravioli and other stuffed pasta dishes did not originate in Sicily; they were in fact northern Italian innovations, yet still dependent upon the Arab introduction of durum wheat. If Persia, with its stuffed wheat dishes, was the origin of *jiaozi* (and the Russian pelmeni), it may also have been a separate and later influence on ravioli in Genoa. However, even if the influence did come later, it is unlikely that Marco Polo could have had anything to do with the improvement of Genoese cooking, unless he taught his lady jailer how to stuff *jiaozi* when he was not busy dictating to Rustichello.

In 1969 and 1970, two articles were published, one in Taiwan by Yan-shuan Lao and one in Wiesbaden by Professor Herbert Franke. Both analysed the vocabulary of a Mongol imperial dietary compendium called the *Yinshan zhengyao*, translated by Yan-shuan Lao as the 'propriety and essentials of beverage and meals'. Though extracting the original term from the Chinese translation was not simple, partly because 'a Mongolian word might be a Turkish loan-word in Mongolian, or a Turkic form which is a borrowing from Persian or Arabic, or rather from Arabic via Persian,' Herbert Franke concluded, 'it should be noted that the words for noodles, ravioli and similar flour-based dishes are all Turkic. This points to the fact that the dishes themselves were originally non-Chinese . . . This would mean that even such dishes as *jiaozi,* which have become a staple and a household feature in Chinese cuisine, might have come to China from the "western barbarians"'.

Ice-cream is another contentious issue. Legend has it that Marco Polo saw ice-cream being made in China and brought the recipe back to Europe.[8] However, the legend appears to be nineteenth-century in origin, as there is nothing in the *Description of the World* that could be construed as a reference to ice-cream. When Robin Weir was checking what would only be a sentence or two in the introduction to his definitive work on ice-cream, he asked me about Marco Polo and in doing so provided one of the many inspirations to continue my work on him. Talking to Robin and researching the question of ice-cream, it became clear that it was likely that the Chinese of the Tang dynasty (618–907) knew how to freeze milk products. A poem of the late twelfth century appears to celebrate ice-cream, as 'greasy-looking yet firmly textured, like jade at the bottom of a dish but melting in the sun'.[9] Nonetheless, the production of ice and the knowledge of methods of lowering temperatures below that of the freezing point of water are quite complicated and seem only to have been successfully investigated by European scientists in the sixteenth century, quite some time after Marco Polo died. In fact, water ices and ice-cream only began to be manufactured in Europe in the seventeenth century.

It is possible that the Arabs also played a part in the transmission of ice-making, although it took a further 300 years for European scientists to understand the secret, for it is recorded in a thirteenth-century Arab medical work.[10] As with pasta, ice-cream can be seen to antedate Marco Polo by more than 300 years. In this case, the connections were made long after the event and have nothing to do with Marco Polo's book or the few known facts about his life. He simply forms, yet again, a convenient bridge between two vastly different and distant civilisations, soaring over the crucial culinary crucible of Persia.

10

Walls within walls

Marco Polo's description of places in China and beyond form, perhaps, his most lasting contribution to our knowledge of the East in the thirteenth century. The first, traditionally 'eyewitness', account of the great cities of China is of especial significance because many of the places he describes have either vanished, like the Mongol summer capital of Shangdu, or been transformed almost beyond recognition, as is the case with today's high-rise Peking. The defeat of the Mongol dynasty in 1368 and the recapture of China by the (Chinese) Ming emperor (whose origins were more obscure than, though just as poverty-stricken as those of Qinghis Khan) involved the destruction of the Mongol capital, Peking, and many other centres that offered resistance. The fall of the Ming dynasty itself in 1644, when the Manchu Qing dynasty took power, involved the re-flattening of Peking and many other cities. In the mid nineteenth century, a Christian-inspired rebellion attempting to establish the *Taiping tianguo* (Kingdom of Heavenly Peace) destroyed much of the Yangtse delta area, including many parts of Yangzhou, Nanjing, Suzhou and Hangzhou. Even today, the old quarters of many of China's prettiest towns are being razed to construct office tower-blocks. So Marco

Polo's description of the glories of Hangzhou and Suzhou remains when their buildings and bridges are disappearing.

Apart from deliberate destruction, a major problem for anyone wishing to reconstruct China's architectural heritage is that almost all Chinese buildings were constructed using timber as the main structural material; and where armies, whether imperial or rebellious, failed, the ravages of weather and time have effectively succeeded. In the case of significant temples, when these fell down they were normally rebuilt, again using timber, on the same spot. Unlike the Japanese, who have, in the case of certain eighth-century temples, demonstrated an extreme reverence for the original, replacing every damaged scrap of timber with an identical replica,[1] Chinese temples were usually rebuilt in the current style. Thus, a temple described as dating back to the third century and seeming nicely traditional is probably a nineteenth-century structure at best, and its bracketing and roof finials are probably in the nineteenth-century rather than the third-century style.

Certain structures, constructed of more durable material, do survive and may be compared with Polo's account; and some cities, like Hangzhou, have been studied through comparisons between Polo's version and contemporary Chinese texts. His descriptions of the layout of Peking, for example, re-create a recognisable city whose chessboard pattern is still evident in places (although construction of three ring roads and the now ubiquitous tower blocks is fast erasing a city that still remained traditional in parts into the late 1980s).

Marco Polo's description of Peking, the newly built capital of Qubilai, is very full. He describes the earthen ramparts surrounding the city, 'built in the form of a square' and 'all battlemented and whitewashed'.[2] These earthen ramparts can still be seen along Xueyuan lu to the north of the city, and they enclosed an enormous amount of land within their twenty-four-mile circumference, stretching far further to the north than the subsequent Ming and Qing cities, though the form of the enclosure was rectangular rather than square as Marco Polo insists. It is generally thought that the enclosure of land beyond the built-up sections of the city was a reflection of the atavistic Mongol desire to remain close to large herds of horses, camels and sheep, whilst the later inhabitants of the city saw the wall as enclosing the city proper rather than grazing land.

The outer city walls do not seem ever to have been battlemented and the reference to whitewash is also puzzling, though both these statements may have simple explanations. Chinese city walls were built on a core of rammed earth and sometimes faced with grey bricks, like those that can still be seen on the surviving city gates in Peking. The mention of battlements may be a rhetorical flourish to emphasise the grandeur of these high and solid rammed earth walls, but, aside from the difficulty of whitewashing earth on this scale, white is not a colour associated with battlements and city walls in China or elsewhere. The only painted walls in Peking today are the dark red walls of the Forbidden City. As Chinese designs were known to have been used by the Mongols in the construction of the new capital city of Peking, whitewash remains unlikely but perhaps, again, the glory of the sight overcame the writer.

The layout of the city of Peking is described as seen from the high city walls: 'the streets are so broad and straight that from the top of the wall above one gate you can see along the whole length of the road to the gate opposite.' Between these broad avenues 'the whole interior of the city is laid out in squares like a chessboard' with the plots of land allocated to housing 'square and measured by the rule'; and 'on every site stand large and capacious mansions with ample courtyards and gardens.'[3] The main roads were lined with shops. This description perfectly accords with traditional Chinese city planning and with the style of the later city of Peking. The city described in the *Description of the World* was destroyed at the fall of the Mongols and it was not until the early fifteenth century that the second Ming emperor decided to relocate the capital on the site, though with some misgivings that the 'good luck' (*fengshui*) of the place had been exhausted by its destruction. This later Ming city was also laid out on a chessboard pattern, but was situated slightly to the south of the Mongol city.

Because of the impermanence of timber and the regular destruction by armies and rebellions, almost all Chinese architectural history is conducted in reverse, looking at what survives and recreating the past by means of scarce reference. Marco Polo's account of Peking is a recreation of a vanished city, but one which is credibly in accord with the way the Chinese liked to build. From the Shang dynasty (*c.* sixteenth century BC to *c.* 1066 BC) on, cities were ideally rectangular and walled, with the palace of the ruler at the centre, again in a rectangular walled enclosure. Streets and avenues were straight, and houses were enclosed in their own walls on regular plots delineated by the street layout. Only shops, which lined the main streets, turned outwards, open to the street; everything else was walled and secret. From the earliest times, beliefs about the 'lucky' siting of buildings were based on the system known as *fengshui* (wind and water) or geomancy. Geomantic practitioners consulted obscure manuals with titles like *The Secrets of the Blue Bag* (universe)[4] and employed special compasses to determine auspicious dates and sites for graves and important buildings. Within a city, the plots were predetermined by the street layout; thus the courtyard houses behind their high walls could be built without recourse to a geomancer, but the site of the city itself was always justified with reference to geomancers. Cities and houses faced south, ideally with a supply of water running in front of the building or city. The construction of cities on the Peking plain was easy, for watercourses could be led from the Yongding river through the city and the flat land, which meant no geomantic problems arose. By contrast, in south China, the city of Nanjing, has irregular walls pressed against hills, which created far greater problems for traditional city planners than flat Peking.

The regularity of the street plan of Peking, as compared with that of cities of the hilly south, means that even today it is very easy to orient oneself by the points of the compass. Street directions are generally not given as 'left' or 'right' but north, south, east or west, so that you might be told to go north for two blocks and find the building you require on the west side of the street. (Such is the force of the orientation of the city that I have even heard a Peking resident identify his overcoat hanging on a row of pegs as 'the one to the west'.)

Though Marco Polo did not describe domestic architecture in any detail, and could probably not have penetrated behind the high walls of the courtyard houses, one detail is of particular significance, as it may refer specifically to Mongol building plans. Describing the gardens of Qubilai Khan's palace, he notes that 'the grass grows here in abundance, because all the paths are paved and built up fully two cubits above the level of the ground, so that no mud forms on them and no rain-water collects in puddles, but the moisture trickles over the lawns...'[5] The stress on grass is interesting, for expanses of grass or lawns have not been part of the later traditional Chinese culture of gardens. Grass is, by contrast, ruthlessly eliminated as it is said to harbour mosquitoes. (I spent many afternoons eliminating grass in the last year of the Cultural Revolution, one type of compulsory manual labour that rather upset the lawn-loving British students.) For the Mongols, however, coming from expansive grasslands, grass was probably an attractive feature in a courtyard.

It is possible that the raised paths he mentions also represent a particularly Mongol architectural feature. Typically, Chinese courtyards might have raised walks around their perimeter but not usually across the centre, whilst one of

85

the few surviving Mongol temples in China, the Yongle gong (or Palace of Eternal Joy) near Ruicheng in Shanxi province, reveals very high, raised walkways through the centre of the main courtyards. The same plan was seen in the remains of a Mongol period courtyard house excavated from beneath one of the Ming dynasty city walls in Peking. Marco Polo does not make it clear that the raised walkways run through the centre of the grassy areas, but to ensure an even spread of rainwater on the grass, it is quite likely that this was what he meant.

Marco Polo's description of the great palace of the Khan, which has completely disappeared, razed by the Ming as a symbol of their conquest, stresses the formal aspect. He describes banquets held in vast halls which could seat 6000, and the rituals associated with Mongol entertainment. The walls of the great halls were adorned with gold and silver and scenes of animals and their pursuit, their roofs ablaze with 'scarlet and blue and green and yellow and all the colours that are'.[6] His account steps beyond the fabulous in his description of the storehouses and congeries of apart-ments and passages at the rear of the palace. He says 'the number of chambers is quite bewildering',[7] and notes that the rear apartments where the women live are closed to outsiders. This arrangement, which was followed in the Ming and Qing imperial palace in Peking, was traditionally Chinese. Private apartments were sited at the rear of court-yard enclosures whilst the great halls for public celebrations were near the main gate, and outsiders or non-family mem-bers were not allowed to penetrate deep into the enclosure.

Like the Khan's palace, certain structures are described in considerable detail, but one of these still stands. This is a bridge in the outskirts of Peking which is still known to tour guides and foreign visitors as 'the Marco Polo bridge'. An elegant construction, it is of particular interest for, unlike the wooden palace and temples which have either been destroyed for ever or totally rebuilt so often as to be unrecognisable except by site, it has survived from the thirteenth century to the present day.

It lies sixteen kilometres west of Peking, over the river now known as the Yongding, but which was previously known as the Lugou. Marco Polo's term for it, *pulisanghin*, is either Persian for 'stone bridge' or Sino-Persian for 'Sanggan bridge' (an earlier name for the river was Sanggan). He describes it as lying ten miles from Peking 'toward the sun-setting' and being either three hundred or four hundred paces long and eight or nine paces wide (the amounts vary-ing in different manuscripts); he continues, 'it has twenty-four arches and twenty-four piers in the water supporting them and it is all of grey marble very well-worked and well-founded. There is above on each side of the bridge a beauti-ful curtain or wall of flags of marble and of pillars artificially made [in Ramusio only] . . .'.[8] He describes pillars with stone lions supporting them, which sound like the stelae normally supported upon stone tortoises that were frequently erected at special places:

> And on either side of the bridge are many small pillars and under each pillar as if for its base is a stone lion and likewise above its head another lion [these details only appear in a Latin compendium of the early fifteenth century now in Ferrara], and from one pillar to the other it is closed in with a flag of grey marble all worked with different sculptures and mortised into the columns at the side [Ramusio only] and so there are altogether on the said bridge 600 pillars with 1200 stone lions on one side and the other of the bridge, and all these are of very fine marble [14th century Latin version only].[9]

The bridge today has only eleven arches and Chinese records indicate that it never had more than thirteen; cer-tainly never twenty-four. Yule contemplated the possibility that Marco Polo was remembering another bridge, to the west, on the Liuli river. However, the notes to Yule's third

edition include information provided by the Reverend Mr
Ament to the effect that there was not a bridge on the Liuli
river until 1522;[10] so we are back with the original bridge
and the assumption that, if he saw it, Marco Polo had either
forgotten the details or was exaggerating again.

The surviving stone bridge was built in 1189–92, restored
in 1444, and again in 1698. It has 120 balusters with small
lions carved at the top (though not at the base) and its
intermediate 'flags' are plain. At either end of the bridge is
a carved stone elephant nudging the end of the parapet
with its forehead. As few details survive of the restoration
work, it is possible that the elephants are a later addition.
If we divide the number of arches, ignore the omission of
elephants and the apparent substitution of stelae-bearing
tortoises by lions, divide his numbers of small lions considerably (removing those at the base of the pillars for they do
not tally with Chinese bridge-building styles), ignore the
Persian name for the site and, as Moule did, compile a
description from a variety of manuscripts in different languages, then the description is passable.

One feature of urban land use in Peking mentioned by
Marco Polo that appears to contrast strongly with later practice was that official 'acts of violence', assumed to mean
public executions, were apparently performed outside the
city walls, in the agricultural suburbs.[11] In later periods, it
was common to hold executions in the most public place
possible to get the message across to the largest number of
people. Under the Qing (1644–1911), executions in Peking
were performed in the vegetable market, so that instead of
saying 'Go hang', the inhabitants would say 'Go to the vegetable market'. Given this later preference for public punishment, it would seem surprising, by contrast, for the Mongols,
whose violent reputation made all Europe tremble, to exhi-
bit a sudden delicacy and conduct their executions at a
decent distance from the public gaze.

Other cities written about at length in the *Description of*

the World include Suzhou, the 'Venice of China', and Hangzhou, the beautiful lakeside city that had served as temporary capital to the southern Song (1127–1279).

Suzhou, in Jiangsu province, was one of the prettiest cities
in China. Lying in the lush, green Yangtse delta, the 'land
of fish and rice' where bright green paddy fields were wat-
ered by the thousands of streams and canals that criss-
crossed the plain, it managed for centuries to combine economic significance with tranquil elegance. The Grand
Canal, the great waterway first constructed in the seventh
century to take rice from the fertile south northwards, runs
through the edge of the city, which was famous for its handicraft production. Silk, produced in the surrounding countryside, was woven in Suzhou and was popular for clothing
amongst the dandies of the thirteenth century (and later).
Much of the handicraft production was of the highest quality
for, from the tenth century, Suzhou was the favoured place
of residence for retired government officials and scholars,
who adorned their pretty houses with fine hardwood furni-
ture, the appurtenances of the scholar's table, paintings and
carvings. The gardens of Suzhou are still famous today
and, though most date from the Ming (1368–1644) or later,
the earliest are of Song foundations. Building a Chinese
garden required a whole series of service industries for,
apart from plants, they were decorated with carved stone
inscriptions, pebbled paths and rockeries of complex construction. Rockery builders, often working with huge lumps
of stone brought by canal from Lake Tai, some fifty kilometres away, became well-paid experts; and architectural
features in houses and gardens, elegant pavilions, carved
wooden interior screens and intricate carved-brick scenes
above gateways were produced by a growing band of highly-
skilled workers.

Marco Polo describes Suzhou as a silk-producing centre,
whose inhabitants were fine craftsmen and merchants, something of a shorthand account, but he did also mention one

of the most notable features of the town: its 'fully 6,000 stone bridges, such that one or two galleys could readily pass beneath them'.[12] Suzhou's streets often ran beside narrow canals, where women washed clothes and vegetables and which were traversed by tiny stone bridges. On the broader Grand Canal, there were numerous elegant stone 'jade-belt' bridges, dramatically high, slim, single-arched stone constructions whose shadows completed perfect belt-like circles reflected in the water below and which allowed the passage of loaded canal boats. Not quite doing the pretty town justice, but as most of its waterways and bridges were narrow and small scale, perhaps it was not terribly impressive to a Venetian, Marco Polo also stated that Suzhou was a market for ginger and rhubarb grown in the mountains nearby. However, there are no mountains as such nearby, for Suzhou lies in the flat, wet Yangtse delta area, and ginger is mainly grown further west. Moreover, rhubarb is certainly not produced near Suzhou and never has been. What Yule calls 'the great rhubarb mart' was at another Suzhou in Gansu province.[13]

Though Suzhou is today sometimes compared to Venice, Marco Polo applied that appellation to Hangzhou (Kinsai, Quinsai), a town near the Qiantang river, edged by the Grand Canal and set beside the great West Lake.[14] It is possible that Marco Polo reversed the cities, for only Suzhou is truly criss-crossed by canals like the smaller waterways of Venice, although the broader expanses of water in the vicinity of Hangzhou are closer in scale (though not scenery) to the Rialto. Marco Polo spoke of 12,000 bridges in Hangzhou, a claim which worried Colonel Yule, for 'Wassaf speaks of 360 bridges only',[15] but in Polo's defence, we know he was considered prone to exaggeration, and his vast number was repeated (or perhaps copied) by Friar Odoric of Pordenone.

The attraction of Suzhou lay in its private gardens, elegant houses, bridges and temples, perhaps too Chinese in spirit for many foreign visitors. Marco Polo's longer description of Hangzhou and his evident greater appreciation of this city was echoed in the enthusiasm of members of the first British embassy to China, who found the great open lake, set by rolling hills dotted with elegant pagodas, an attractively landscaped sight, much to the eighteenth-century English taste.

The lake at Hangzhou, surrounded by temples and grand mansions, said Polo, who made no note of the extraordinary rocket-shaped Bao Chu pagoda (restored in 1003), was covered with brightly painted flat-bottomed pleasure barges, poled slowly about so that diners could enjoy a lavish meal (in the company of 'their womenfolk or hired women') at the same time as feasting 'their eyes on the diversity and beauty of the scenes through which they are passing',[16] a familiar description to contemporary tourists who have been steered slowly about the lake and supplied with bottles of fizzy orangeade, but no hired women.

Marco Polo the merchant stressed the handicraft production in Hangzhou, organised by craft guilds and practised in distinct quarters of the city. Some of the fullest descriptions of the handicraft quarters, where it was still traditional for sons to be compelled to follow their father's craft, and where wealth was demonstrated in the silken gowns and jewels worn by the wives of the best craftsmen, occur only in the Ramusio version. Hangzhou's ten great markets (again only in Ramusio) attracted 40,000 to 50,000 customers, according to Polo, who purchased fresh fish, caught in the West Lake or brought upriver from the seaside. They enjoyed huge pears 'weighing ten pounds apiece, white as dough inside and very fragrant',[17] which sound like the strange Tianjin pears you can buy today which have a white, crisp, but juice-filled flesh, unlike our pears, which are either hard and juiceless or soft and lacking a distinctive crunchiness. Large they may have been, but the weight given by Polo must be another of his famous multiplications.

These, apart from grapes and raisins (imported), are the only fruits mentioned by name. In addition, his description of the meat available is strangely Islamic. Moule remarked on the absence of pork from the lists of produce in the meat market (dog-meat is included); and, noting that pork was specifically mentioned by Odoric of Pordenone, suggested: 'Probably Mark may have got a little Saracenized among the Mohammedans at the Khan's court.'[18]

Other aspects of daily life in Hangzhou which Marco Polo mentioned include the public bath-houses, multi-storeyed houses, and the consequent danger of fire. Bathing customs varied throughout China but southern China was more prone to washing than the west or north. Much earlier, it had apparently been customary for officials to bathe and wash their hair at home every ten days, so that salaries were called 'emoluments of the bath and hair-washing', and government servants had a day off every ten days for their ablutions.[19] Since the upper classes presumably still bathed at home, the bath-houses that Marco Polo mentioned were probably used by ordinary people. They seem to have been places where time could be spent, tea drunk and massages of all sorts provided, as indeed they still are at public bath-houses in China. Marco Polo states that the normal water used was brought cold from the lake, but foreigners could have hot water baths. Other visitors noted them (a Japanese visitor in the eleventh century carefully taking down the prices listed at the door, which was marked by the sign of a large jar) and, like the great baths of Turkey, for example, they were unmissable from the lines of pedlars selling soap and other bathing requisites, including patent lotions and medicines, that lined the approach to the bath-house itself.

Foreigners described the houses of Hangzhou at the time as being multi-storeyed, beautifully decorated with carved wood and crammed together. Arab travellers mentioned houses of three to five storeys, but Odoric of Pordenone (slightly afflicted by the same tendency to exaggerate as

Marco Polo) described towering dwellings of eight to ten storeys.[20] The description is surprising for it is rare, even in southern China, to find houses or shops of more than two storeys, though two storeys are quite common, especially in the buildings (shop in front and dwelling behind) that line the streets of larger towns in the south. This was not the case in traditional Peking, for the capital of China was dismissed by Lord Stanley in the mid nineteenth century: 'Peking's a gigantic failure, isn't it? Not a single two-storeyed house in the whole place, eh?'[21] That Hangzhou probably did have multi-storeyed houses in the late Song and Yuan periods, despite the fact that this was not remarked upon in Chinese accounts, is borne out by the census figures, for it was unlikely that a million people could have crammed into the walled area hemmed in by lake and hills without recourse to high-rise dwellings.[22]

Packed wooden houses raised the danger of fire, and many of China's cities had early established fire-fighting teams, which were equipped with hatchets, buckets, fire-proof clothing, ropes and ladders to fight blazes and watch-towers, which signalled the location and severity of a fire by means of flags.[23] Marco Polo's account of fire-fighting in Mongol Hangzhou is slightly different from the practices known for the preceding Song dynasty, and suggests that the Mongol administration (which used drums rather than flags for signalling) was extremely strict in its control of the population. Polo also mentioned the construction of tall stone or brick store-houses in which valuables were kept for their protection. There is a stone tower in the Confucian family mansion in Qufu (Shandong province),[24] which was used to protect belongings and people when the mansion was attacked, and small towns in the Canton area often used such towers when pirates attacked.

The wealth of detail in the *Description of the World* of Hang-zhou's markets, pleasure boats on the lake, the temples in the surrounding hills, the handicraft workshops (their products, alas, not described), the bath-houses, the fire-service and the elaborately dressed merchants' wives creates a lively picture of a flourishing city, apparently largely unaffected by the fall of the southern Song in 1279. Marco Polo's description was used, in conjunction with many Chinese texts, to create a full picture of daily life in China in the late thirteenth century,[25] for much of what is contained in the *Description of the World* is borne out by the Chinese sources.

Marco Polo's description of Quanzhou (Zayton, Zalton) is, by comparison, inadequate. He described it, accurately, as one of the two greatest seaports in the world, for it was from Quanzhou that much of China's overseas trade was shipped: boatloads of green celadon vessels, white porcelain and silks bound for South-East Asia and Japan. Marco Polo mainly specified the return cargoes of gems and pearls from India, although the bulk of the cargoes seems in fact to have consisted of spices, precious woods and medicinal ingredients. At the time, it was also one of the major centres of Islam in China, with a Muslim Inspector of Customs, an honorary title conferred on the Arab or Persian merchant who imported the greatest quantities of frankincense, and a fine mosque, built in 1009. In the outskirts are the tombs of two Muslim sages who were said to have come to the city during the Tang dynasty (618–907), yet Polo, who usually knew his Muslims from his Buddhists, described it as a city of (Buddhist) idolators, ignoring also the fine Manichaean temple nearby. The river is wrongly described as a tributary of the Qiantang river that flows by Hangzhou, and the brevity of the description suggests either a lack of personal contact or, given his merchant background, a surprising lack of interest.

Yangzhou, which, according to one manuscript he governed for three years, is again, surprisingly, only described as a major administrative centre, producing horse trappings with 'nothing else here worthy of note'.[26] Even the Japanese

Railway Guide of 1924 is more enthusiastic: 'The place has always been known as one of pleasure and gaiety . . . In the palmy days of Yangzhou, it was said that a man having once entered the city in search of pleasure would find himself unable to leave it until he had squandered his all.' Yangzhou's city walls were skirted by the Grand Canal (along which the seventh-century Sui emperor travelled in a barge pulled by teams of beautiful girls) and, like Hangzhou, though the major sources of local wealth were silk, rice and salt, it was also a handicraft centre where the necessaries of elegant life were produced. Like Suzhou, it was a place where the rich chose to live, building pretty house-garden complexes. Though most of those that survive today are much later (as is Yangzhou's fame as the home of the eight 'eccentric' eighteenth-century painters who used their pigtails and fingernails as brushes or hurled splashes of ink at paper to create dotty landscapes), at least one of the famous gardens had been built in 1048 by the poet Ouyang Xiu. Ouyang Xiu, who sat in his high Mountain-flattening Hall to drink and write poetry, was a Governor of Yangzhou in the eleventh century, an illustrious predecessor of Marco Polo.

11

He missed
the biggest wall

Though Marco Polo's descriptions of places and buildings range from the full and elaborate description of Hangzhou to the brief and unsatisfactory accounts of Quanzhou and Yangzhou, one massive construction that he failed to mention was the Great Wall. At first sight, this omission seems particularly damning, but the issue is complicated by the question of what the Great Wall might have looked like in the thirteenth century and how much of it actually existed at the time.

Whether looking at a map of China today, flying over the north of China, or arriving on the Trans-Siberian railway, only someone who is severely visually challenged could fail to notice the Great Wall and, indeed, be very impressed by it. It is generally acknowledged as one of the wonders of the world, snaking back and forth for thousands of miles over the hills of northwestern China. Arguments still continue as to its length with estimates ranging from 24,482 to 31,250 miles.[1] These vary largely because of the way the Wall was built, over centuries and over varied terrain with double interior walls in some sections. Despite its unarguably tremendous length and its considerable breadth (wide enough for four cavalrymen to ride abreast along the eastern sections), the most recent myth about the Wall is quite without foundation. It has been said that it is the only man-made structure visible to the naked eye from the moon: but although dramatic in length, it simply is not wide enough to be seen from the moon.

Based on smaller earlier, walls, and demonstrating the age-old Chinese love of enclosure (keeping strangers out of their houses, keeping people in their places), the Great Wall was first constructed during the reign of the Qin emperor Shi huangdi, who reigned from 221 BC to 206 BC and who is better known for the immense mausoleum with its side pits filled with a 'buried army' of larger-than-life terracotta warriors that he created for himself near Xi'an. Qin Shi huangdi was clearly keen on massive public works built by soldiers and citizens, who were compelled to do manual service as part of their tax payment to the state, constructing roads and walls throughout his empire. His Great Wall linked and extended existing walls which had been built to protect the separate 'warring' states that occupied the north of China until his conquest and unification of the territory in 221 BC.

During the subsequent Han dynasty (206 BC to AD 220), when the Chinese empire extended its control westwards across the Gobi desert, the Wall was extended, too, and garrisons were installed to maintain the signal beacons and defend the Wall. At this time, the Wall was probably constructed in the main from earth. For thousands of years the Chinese have used the 'yellow earth' of north-west China to construct city walls, houses, palaces and towers. The method of construction remains the same today: earth is shovelled in between frames of planks and pounded down in layers creating remarkably long-lasting walls and plat-forms. (I spent a happy week in the autumn of 1975 building walls for winter greenhouses in the Peking suburbs this way.)

It was not until the Ming (1368–1644), some decades after the Polos' visit, that parts of the Wall, including the sections nearest the capital, were faced with brick. The solid

structure that resulted can be found near Peking at Bada-
ling, where most tourists now see it. Today it is one of the
things that every tourist in China wants to see and its renown
in Europe stretches back to the eighteenth century and
beyond. Dr Johnson commented on it in 1778.

> He talked with an uncommon animation of travelling into
> distant countries; that the mind was enlarged by it, and
> that an acquisition of dignity of character was derived
> from it. He expressed a particular enthusiasm with respect
> to visiting the wall of China. I catched it for the moment
> and said I really believed that I should go and see the
> wall of China, had I not children of whom it was my duty
> to take care. 'Sir (said he) by doing so you would do
> what would be of importance in raising your children to
> eminence. There would be a lustre reflected on them
> from your spirit and curiosity. They would be at all times
> regarded as the children of a man who had gone to visit
> the wall of China. I am serious, Sir.[2]

It is possible that Johnson derived his impression of the Wall
from Diderot's *Encyclopaedia* (1765) where it was compared
favourably with the pyramids of Egypt.

The Ming Wall also greatly impressed the members of
Lord Macartney's first British embassy to China.

> What the eye could, from a single spot, embrace of those
> fortified walls, carried along the ridges of hills, over the
> tops of the highest mountains, descending into the deep-
> est vallies, crossing upon arches over river, and doubled
> and trebled in many parts to take in important passes, and
> interspersed with towers or massy bastions at almost every
> hundred yards, as far as the sight could reach, presented
> to the mind an undertaking of stupendous magnitude.[3]

Having studied all the available books on China before
embarking on the embassy, Lord Macartney's secretary,

Staunton was perhaps the first to raise the difficult problem of Marco Polo's failure to record it:

> The first European who published any account of that empire, Marco Polo, has made, however, no mention of the wall; tho as he travelled over land to the capital of China, it is presumed he must have passed through it from Tartary in some spot where the wall now stands. From such silence some doubts have arisen . . . whether the wall was really in existence in the thirteenth century.[4]

Apart from his suggestion that the Wall might not yet have been in existence, Staunton made one of the first major defences of Polo's 'silence' by suggesting that it was an editorial mistake which could have been rectified, had he 'given to the world a regular account of his travels immediately on his return, instead of the unconnected fragments which he dictated long afterwards, at a distance from his own home, and separated, as he was probably, from the notes taken on the spot, and other [sic] his original papers'. He continues the defence by citing a copy of the Polo's route to China 'taken from the Doge's library at Venice' which reveals that

> after having followed the usual track of the caravans, as far to the eastward from Europe as Samarcand and Cashgar, he bent his course to the southeast across the river Ganges to Bengal; and keeping to the southward of the Thibet mountains, reached the Chinese province of Shensee [Shaanxi], and through the adjoining province of Shansee [Shanxi] to the capital, without interfering with the line of the great wall.[5]

However, this route would suggest a detour of some 5,000 kilometres as the crow flies and include some of the roughest and most inhospitable terrain in the world; even allowing for the years that the Polos spent on their travels, this would have lengthened their voyage enormously.

Staunton also mentioned the possibility that the Great Wall simply was not there at the time, and this argument has been repeated recently. It is thought by some that it might have fallen into such a state of disrepair between the Qin and the Ming as to have all but disappeared.[6] Part of the evidence of this lies in the lack of mention of wall-building or wall-repairing activities in some of the imperial histories, most notably of the Tang (618–906) and Song (960–1279) dynasties. For the Tang emperors, whose capital was situated far south-west of Peking in today's Xi'an, there was no great need to strengthen the Wall: the perceived threats to the Tang came from the west, not the north, and, at times of difficulty, they simply moved their capital further to the south-east, to Luoyang.

As the Song court was constantly threatened by Altaic peoples from the north, it could be argued that they should have paid more attention to threats from the north, and therefore have strengthened the Wall. In 1050, the Xixia or Tangut conquered Chinese territory around Ningxia in the north-west, and the Liao, a Mongolian-speaking group, controlled the north-east and had their capital at Peking (whose name in Chinese, Beijing, means 'northern capital'; though the Liao, coming from further north, rather confusingly renamed the city Nanjing or 'southern capital').

In 1122, the Liao were deposed by another Altaic group, the Jurchens, whose linguistic affiliations were Tungusic rather than Mongolian. The Jurchens founded the Jin dynasty and moved southwards, forcing the Song court to move its capital from Kaifeng southwards to Hangzhou in 1127. Although the Wall functioned not so much as a physical barrier (for it could not keep out a determined army) but as a provider of communication lines and shelter for border guards, attention to the maintenance of a garrison on the Wall might have prevented this southern flight.

Interestingly, the Jin, who traversed the Great Wall (if it existed then) with ease, devoted some effort to wall-building. Waldron states, 'The Mongols encountered no Great Wall when they conquered China', though he notes that they were 'briefly held up at Juyongguan [a pass on the Wall now marked by a spectacular gateway carved with multi-lingual inscriptions built by the Mongols themselves in 1354] by the Jin who had strengthened their bastion impressively'.[7] In his first sentence, the words are carefully chosen. The Mongols were certainly not held back by the Great Wall for it was not the Wall itself, easy to scale if undefended, that impeded invasion, but its defence by border guards. The fact that they were not impeded need not imply that the Wall did not exist, simply that, undefended, it was not a military barrier. Similarly, the Manchus, another Tungusic group from the far north-east, swept across the better fortified (but temporarily undefended) Ming Wall to found the Qing dynasty in 1644.

Though it is certain that the brick-facing of the Wall, which makes the sections to the north and north-east of Peking so striking today, was done after the Polos travelled east, much of the Wall was, and still is, made of yellow earth. The earthen sections are much narrower than the brick-faced sections, but they are still striking when seen, for example, from the train across the desert from Xi'an to Dunhuang. Elsewhere, the survival of tamped earth city walls in China is usually dramatic: parts of the Shang dynasty (from *c.* sixteenth century BC to 1066 BC) city walls can still be seen in Zhengzhou. My feeling is that even without serious wall-building or wall-repairing efforts, there would have been much of the tamped earth wall surviving in the thirteenth century and that it would have been very difficult to have travelled into China from the West without noticing it; thus the omission of the Wall in the *Description of the World* is telling.

12

Not unique and certainly not a siege engineer

One of Marco Polo's claims was that he, his father and his uncle were the first 'Latins' ever seen by Qubilai Khan. *'Il avait tres grande joie de leur venue çomme un qui n'a jamais vu aucun Latin'* (He was greatly pleased by their arrival as he had never seen an Italian). The German Mongolist Professor Franke noted that this 'is another statement in this book that is open to doubt', and quoted a passage from the Chinese annals for 1260–61 when a group of Europeans, described as *'falang'* or Franks (the name by which all Europeans were known in the Near East), arrived at the Khan's summer palace at Shangdu.[1] It was reported that they came from a country of constant day-light, possibly Novgorod, and that they could only tell when evening came when field mice emerged. The people were fair and blue-eyed and local insects such as flies and mosquitoes were born from wood. A somewhat mysterious group, they were nevertheless sufficiently important to be recorded in the official annals.

William of Rubruck, who had arrived in Karakorum in 1254, was, like Marco Polo, not mentioned in the official annals of the Mongol era, but from his account of life there, a picture of a surprisingly large and varied European community can be formed.[2] The community included a Parisian jeweller and an Englishman named Basil. Thus, although it is possible that the Polos were the first Italians in the Mongol capital, they were certainly not the first foreigners, and not even the first Europeans seen by the Mongols.

The Mongols' association with outsiders and their well-documented 'use' of non-Mongol experts is possibly based in their nomadic tradition. Moving with their herds from summer to winter pastures, they developed skills in horsemanship and animal husbandry, but were compelled to trade with their sedentary neighbours, exchanging furs and meat for essential metal weapons and luxury goods like textiles and tea, products of the settled agricultural life of the Chinese. When Qinghis Khan subdued the other tribes of Mongolia, it was his practice to incorporate their soldiers into the Mongol army.[3] The skills and techniques of other local peoples were also drawn upon. The first writing system for Mongolian was borrowed, adapted from Uighur Turkish during Qinghis' reign, and the second, the 'Phags-pa script, was derived from the Tibetan script and made compulsory in 1269.[4]

With their expansion across Asia, the Mongols' way of life began to change. Rather than the movable settlements of tents which were rolled up and transported to different grazing sites according to the season, a more permanent settlement was established in the Mongol heartland, from where the expanding empire was ruled. Descriptions of Qinghis' capital of Karakorum in the thirteenth century indicate that it was a proper settlement rather than a nomads' camp, demonstrating features such as a surrounding wall enclosing separate 'Chinese' and 'Muslim' quarters.[5]

Karakorum was the object of early Christian missions to Mongolia and was described at length by William of Rubruck, who visited it in 1253–54. Previous Christian envoys such as Andrew of Longjumeau, who had been sent by Louis IX in 1249 and returned with a patronising letter requesting annual tribute to the Khan, were unable to leave a record since they failed to reach the city itself; and as mentioned earlier, John of Plano Carpini who was sent by Pope Innocent IV, only reached a camp at some distance from the city, where he stayed from 1246–47.

The city of Karakorum, as finally seen and described by Rubruck, presented very interesting aspects. It had been walled in 1235, although it is clear from John of Plano Carpini's experience that some Mongols still pitched camp outside the walls according to their nomadic tradition. William of Rubruck was not greatly impressed by Karakorum, which he said was smaller than Saint Denis near Paris. Clearly intended to disparage, the comparison is not, perhaps, quite as demeaning as it seems, for Saint Denis was dominated by its magnificent Gothic abbey, the burial place of most of the French kings. Rubruck suggested that if you removed the Khan's palace, Saint Denis would have been the bigger city. As twentieth-century Russian excavations of the walled city of Karakorum have revealed the dominance of the palace,[6] one could equally have said that, without its great church, Saint Denis might have been the smaller settlement.

Within the city, settled life was graced by the presence of a number of foreign experts, some more willing residents than others. There were Nestorian clergymen, looked upon with some hostility by the Franciscan visitor; Chinese craftsmen; Persian architects; a Ruthenian goldsmith; a Greek doctor; Paquette, a Frenchwoman married to a Russian who waited on Mangu Khan's daughter; Basil, son of an Englishman and nephew of a Norman bishop; and the 'Parisian goldsmith' Guillaume Boucher, who invited William of Rubruck for dinner on Palm Sunday, April 5th, 1254.

Boucher was married to a Frenchwoman who had been born in Hungary, and the two of them had been living and working in Belgrade in 1242 when the city was captured by the Mongols and they were taken east to Karakorum, where they were kept as slaves. Despite their low official status, Boucher was esteemed as a metalworker, a craft virtually unknown to the Mongols. Though able to support themselves by herding, the Mongols had always relied upon outsiders for their weapons and other essential metal utensils.

Though, sadly, nothing survives of his delicate craftsmanship, it is probable that Boucher made jewellery for the Mongol nobility, and this would have justified his existence in Karakorum. As a good Christian, William of Rubruck tended only to describe items such as a silver crucifix which, to his horror, was stolen by Nestorian monks who disapproved of idolatry. According to William of Rubruck, still stressing the religious note, Boucher also made an iron pan for the preparation of wafers and a very unusual silver pyx or box for holding the consecrated wafers. William praised a portable altarpiece with an image of the Virgin 'after the French fashion', protected by two hinged doors carved with Gospel stories, and, for once describing in detail an item distinctly non-Christian in inspiration and use, the most spectacular of Boucher's creations: the magical alcohol-dispensing fountain.

All the Mongols' feasts and festivals were marked by the massive consumption of a variety of alcohols: rice wine from China, grape wines from Persia and Turkestan, and the local *kumis*, made from fermented mare's milk, 'in such a way,' as William of Rubruck says, 'that you would take it for white wine'. With the help of fifty assistants, Boucher made a fountain to dispense with elegance the one hundred and fifty cartloads and ninety horse-loads of *kumis* delivered for the average four-day feast. He made a great silver tree with curving branches hung with leaves and fruit of gilded silver, four crouching lions at the base, and an angel blowing a real trumpet at the top of the tree. The branches and the lions had hollow tubes inside them, through which the *kumis* was poured, and the angel's trumpet was blown by a gentleman concealed within the trunk of the tree. (Boucher had hoped that he could create a sort of automatic internal machinery that would work the contraption without human effort, but this had failed and he had had to resort to the concealment of the person inside.[7])

The cosmopolitan nature of the Khan's entourage was repeated after the Mongols established the new capital of Dadu ('great capital') at Peking in 1267. The capital city itself was designed by a Muslim architect.[8] His official title was Director of the Chatie, which is glossed as meaning 'tent' in Mongol (though the term itself was a borrowing from *cadyr*, the word for tent in many Turkic languages); so the imperial director of building was, in fact, in honour of the Mongols' ancestral practices, the Director of Tents.[9] Such archaic titles persist in China today. The word for 'Chairman', as in Chairman Mao, in fact refers not to a person sitting at the head of a table in the most important chair, but to the person occupying the 'principal mat', for until the arrival of chairs in the ninth century the Chinese sat on the floor on mats (a habit borrowed by the Japanese in the eighth century) and the most important person sat on the principal mat.[10]

The plans and buildings of the new capital, though designed by a Muslim architect, were Chinese in influence, apparently because only by using Chinese designs on the most imposing scale did the Mongols feel they could 'over-awe the Chinese people and avoid ridicule'.[11] It goes without saying that the Mongols themselves had no tradition of monumental architecture so they could bring little from their tradition that would overwhelm the Chinese architecturally. Though the designer of the great capital was not awarded a biographical entry in the official history of the Yuan dynasty, he was described in a contemporary record, the *Guizhai wenji* (*Works from the Studio of the Jade Tablet*) by Ouyang Xun (1274–1358).[12]

Early in his career, Qinghis Khan had relied upon Yelu chucai (1189–1243), a Sinicised Khitan, for advice on government. Yelu chucai is often credited with the saying that though the Chinese empire had been conquered on horseback, it could not be ruled from horseback.[13] The Khitan were a semi-nomadic Mongol steppe tribe who founded the short-lived Liao dynasty in north China (907–1125), based just to the north-east of Peking. The Khitan experience of government was reflected in Yelu chucai's advice on taxation of agriculture, internal trade and handicraft production as well as the promotion of mining and industry.[14]

When Qubilai took over China in 1260, he continued to use Chinese advisors, who were accustomed to the Chinese bureaucracy. Turks, who had also worked for the Mongols since the time of Qinghis, continued to serve as generals, local officials, imperial tutors and translators. Central Asian Muslims were brought in to supervise trade, and the Tibetan 'Phags-pa lama, who had invented the writing system named after him, remained a close personal advisor. Envoys were sent to India to seek out medical doctors,[15] Persian doctors and medical works were consulted, and Persians served as court astronomers.

It may be that in insisting upon his father's and uncle's origins as 'Latins', Marco Polo was distinguishing Italians from all other Europeans, but the cosmopolitan mix at Karakorum, together with the embassy of 'Franks', and the linguistic failure to distinguish between different Europeans in Chinese, make it unlikely that Qubilai Khan differentiated between nationalities with such finesse.

Other foreign advisors employed by Qubilai included Korean boat-builders to strengthen the navy, and Ismail and Ala al-Dīn, engineers sent for from Persia to build man-gonels (stone-hurling machines) and huge catapults, both of which were used to break defences during the siege of Xiangyang (1268–73).[16] Xiangyang, on the north bank of the Han river (opposite Fancheng) was one of the last strongholds of the Song dynasty, and the final Mongol victory in 1273 after a five-year siege represented a major turning point in the conquest of China, which was finally achieved in 1279. Many of the non-Chinese experts and advisors, including those who helped to break the Chinese resistance at Xiangyang, are known from their biographies in the official history of the Mongols (the *Yuan shi* or *History of the Yuan*, compiled between 1367 and 1370) and other written sources, but all experts agree that the same works contain absolutely no mention of the Polos.

One of the claims made in the *Description of the World* is that the Polos themselves suggested the construction of mangonels and instructed members of their retinue to produce and demonstrate the weapons. It described the difficulty of taking the city:

> And I assure you that the besiegers would never have taken it but for a circumstance which I will now relate . . . Messer Niccolo and Messer Maffeo and Messer Marco declared: 'We shall find you a means by which the city will be forced to surrender forthwith . . . we have with us in our retinue men who will make mangonels that will hurl such huge stones that the besieged will be unable to endure it' . . . Then Messer Niccolo and his brother and son, who had amongst their retinue a German and a Nestorian Christian who were masters of this art, bade them make two or three mangonels that hurled stones of 300 pounds . . . What more need I say? When the trebuchets were erected and wound up, then one of them hurled a stone into the city. The stone landed on houses, shattering and wrecking everything . . . When the citizens saw this disaster . . . they made up their minds to surrender . . .[17]

Apart from the evidence of the use of Persian military engineers, Marco Polo's claim is easily dismissed, for the siege of Xiangyang was broken a year before the Polos are supposed to have arrived in China.[18] The siege and its breaking are described by Rashīd al-Dīn, who said that there had been no 'Frankish' (European) mangonels in China before the Persian engineers constructed them.[19]

The desire of Marco Polo to associate himself with this famous siege is not unique. His near-contemporary and self-styled fellow-traveller Sir John Mandeville also claimed to have been 'living with the Great Khan for sixteen months' in an echo of Marco Polo's seventeen years,[20] and also said that he served as a soldier in the fight against the Song, though it is quite certain that Mandeville was never in China. He was a plagiarist who freely copied Ordoric of Pordenone's account of China and also used other written accounts such as those of Albert of Aix, Haiton of Armenia, William of Tripoli, Caesarius of Heisterbach and Vincent of Beauvais. No matter what he borrowed, Mandeville invariably placed himself in the forefront of whatever excitement was going on. The fact that his book was an enormous success, at the time as great as that of Marco Polo, perhaps suggests that Marco Polo, too, was not beyond seeking wealth and renown through 'having been there'.

Someone who was definitely 'there' but who does not survive in the popular imagination is Rabban Sauma, a traveller who moved in the opposite direction to the Polos. Very shortly after the great siege of Xiangyang, the Mongol ruler of the Persian Ilkhanate, Arghun, continued the Mongol tradition of using non-Mongols by sending Rabban Sauma, a Nestorian cleric, on a mission to the West in the late 1280s. Rabban Sauma had been born into a Nestorian family in Peking in about 1225 and had travelled to the Holy Land with his young disciple, Mar. When the head of the Nestorian Church in Baghdad died in 1281, Mar was appointed his successor and Rabban Sauma continued his travels alone. In Rome, he was received by the Pope, whom he told of the Nestorian conversion of the Mongols of Persia. Indeed, Arghun's second son, Öljeitü (who succeeded his brother Ghazan and ruled from 1304 to 1316), had been baptised and given the name Nicholas in honour of Pope Nicholas IV.[21]

From Rome, Rabban Sauma travelled to Paris, where he met Philip the Fair (Philip IV, 1268–1314), whose son, Charles of Valois, was to receive one of the first manuscript copies of the *Description of the World* in 1307 from Thibault de Chepoy. Rabban Sauma was shown holy relics including the crown of thorns and a section of the Cross and then journeyed to Gascony, where he met Rustichello's patron, Edward I of England, in 1287. Rabban Sauma recorded Edward's words on hearing of the Nestorian beliefs of Arghun: "We, the king of these cities, have taken the sign of the Cross upon our body and have no other thought than this affair. My heart swells when I learn that what I am thinking is also being thought by King Arghun.'[22] Like the Popes, Edward I hoped that the Persian Mongols, at least, would support European crusading attempts to retake Jerusalem and, indeed, a second Mongol embassy in 1289 offered support with transport problems, though, complicated by papal doubts about supporting unorthodox Nestorians, these promises lapsed when Arghun died in 1291.

In Rabban Sauma, late thirteenth-century Europeans met for the first time a man born in China and familiar with Mongol rulers, a direct envoy from the mysterious East of great potential usefulness. He was, however, above all a cleric and his conversations and impressions were of Christianity and its relics, rather than the military organisation of the Mongols. Despite his knowledge of Peking (which was not transmitted to his religious interlocutors), his familiarity with the Mongols was mainly based in the Persian Ilkhanate, rather than the Mongol heartland or China. Information on those areas and the foreigners in the service of the Mongols was dependent upon the accounts of the Christian envoys like William of Rubruck, or those of travellers like the Polos, demonstrably unreliable given claims of their own uniqueness and their impossible participation in seige-breaking.

13

Who were the Polos?

Marco Polo was not a siege engineer, nor was he the first European to meet the Mongol Khan, and he wandered around China with his eyes alternatively open (to porcelain and palaces) and closed (to ladies' feet, Great Walls and proffered cups of tea).

Marco Polo's book, however full of wonderful descriptions, is also filled with inaccuracies and discrepancies. Some of these have been explained away through the lapse of time and memory, or blamed on his co-author's lack of interest, but some are more problematic and can be interpreted in various ways. Even if Rustichello is blamed for some of the omissions and elisions, and later copyists are blamed for others, the question of why the book came to be written, who Marco Polo was, and what he contributed to the *Description of the World* is difficult to resolve after 500 years and on precious little evidence. The impersonal though occasionally detailed description of places and customs that fills the *Description of the World* suggests that Marco Polo was a man with a lively curiosity and, if the style of the work is not entirely the work of his ghost writer, a descriptive gift.

Apart from interpretation and extrapolation, very little is known about Marco Polo save the bare account in the Prologue to the *Description of the World,* which simply tell us that he lived abroad for twenty-six years and that, in 1298, whilst in prison in Genoa, he wrote down his account of those years. Beyond this simple outline of how the years between 1271 and 1295 were spent, what little information we have about Marco Polo and his family comes from other, secondary sources. There are references in Jacopo da Acqui's *Imago Mundi*;[1] a small number of surviving documents, such as family wills and documents in the Venetian archives recording minor legal battles; and the longest account, unfortunately not entirely reliable, in Giovanni Batista Ramusio's *Navigationi et Viaggi*, published in 1559. Despite the gap between Marco Polo's death in 1324 and the production of *Navigationi et Viaggi*, Ramusio is the most significant influence in the creation of the legend of Marco Polo.

Even Polo's origins are mysterious. Though we traditionally think of him as a Venetian merchant, Marco Polo is also claimed by ex-Yugoslavia as a native of the Dalmatian island of Korčula (or Curzola) which was under Venetian control at the time. The Dalmatian connection is supported by a mid-fourteenth-century manuscript in the British Library which states that the Polos came originally from Dalmatia,[2] but there is no other literary evidence.

Even if we accept that Marco came from Venice, there were, however, various Polo families in Venice and its territories in the thirteenth century; Sir Henry Yule described the difficulties of sorting them out by following Ramusio, whose conclusions would suggest longevity beyond our wildest dreams. To Marco the traveller, the man who only acknowledged three daughters in his will, Ramusio ascribes a mythical son (whose grandson left his property to a woman whose father was born in 1271, but who herself married, and subsequently bore children, in 1414).[3]

We know for certain that there was a family called Polo of the San Geremia district in Venice, which seems to have achieved a high civic status, for a Nicolo Polo of San Geremia was made a member of the Council of Venice in 1381.[4] However, despite the similarity in names, no definite connection between the council member and the travelling Polos has been established. Sir Henry Yule mentioned a Venetian Council minute of 1302 exempting a gentleman (*providis vir*) called Marco Polo from incurring a fine for not having his water pipe inspected but, owing to the apparent status of the gentleman, Yule concluded that this was probably a San Geremia Polo and not the traveller. The situation is exacerbated by Ramusio's confusion of the two families: he described the Polo coat of arms as being three '*pole*' birds on an azure ground, but in fact these arms belonged to the San Geremia Polos. Nevertheless, this did not stop Moule from including a long footnote on whether these *pole* birds were red-legged choughs, black and yellow wading birds, or jackdaws.[5]

It has to be concluded that little is known of Marco Polo's ancestry beyond the generation of his father and uncles, for the only mention of a grandfather, by Ramusio, the creator of the Polo legend, cannot be traced elsewhere.[6] No one is even certain now which of the three brothers was the eldest. From the date of his will it is assumed that Marco the Elder, Marco's uncle, died in about 1280. (According to Ramusio, though, he died early and his name was given to his newly born nephew; however, as his will was made in 1280 – when Marco was about twenty-seven and in the employment of the Great Khan, according to the *Description of the World* – this can be discounted.) Niccolo, Marco's father, died in about 1300 and Maffeo in about 1310.

The three brothers Polo, Marco senior, Maffeo and Niccolo, had formed a 'brotherly company' with trading houses in Constantinople and Soldaia or Sudak on the Crimean coast of the Black Sea.[7] Venice, on Italy's Adriatic coast, was the major port in the trade with Constantinople. The rising European demand for Far Eastern spices and silks was supplied mainly through entrepôts such as Constantinople, for travel further east took traders into unknown territories threatened both by the rise and expansion of Islam and the similarly expanding Mongol empire. Their trading house in Sudak gave the Polos access to a three-way trade that was beginning to develop between Venice, the north and the east. From the ninth century a particular trade pattern emerged that involved northern goods such as salt, iron and Slav slaves acquired through the Crimea being exchanged in Constantinople and Egypt for silks and spices from further east.[8]

In 1260, Marco's father, Niccolo, and one of his uncles, Maffeo Polo, made what was, apparently, their first extensive trip beyond the area which they knew well. They sailed from Venice to Constantinople and then on by boat to Sudak. In these voyages near home they probably used Venetian ships, perhaps still galleys worked by teams of slaves, or the increasingly widely used sailing ships. In the second half of the thirteenth century, sailors were beginning to use primitive compasses for navigation and, in the seas near home, probably used their own navigational handbooks detailing coastlines and shoals, as map making was still in its infancy.

Beyond Sudak, the Polos travelled overland. They may have used horses and donkeys briefly, but probably relied upon camel transport from the Pamirs. Horses were no use as dray animals in the long marches of the Central Asian deserts, where water sources were brackish and far between, and grass impossible to find. Though not used as beasts of burden on these difficult trade routes, horses were widely traded from Mongolia down into northern China and even from Persia into India; the trade was kept up by demand for fine Arab horses amongst the rulers of India and Mongolia, which remained constant. One of the reasons for the high demand was the difficulty in breeding horses of a consistent standard in hot, southern climates, and even China, especially as the local buffaloes and bullocks were more suitable dray animals. Marco Polo's numerous references to fine white horses at the Khan's court in Peking testifies to their continuing import from the Near East.

Unlike horses, the great shaggy, two-humped camels, whose thick hair comes off in handfuls in the spring, were ideally suited to the rocky, sandy terrain eastwards from Persia. Bad-tempered and with a tendency to spit evil-smelling saliva in soaking quantities, they were also difficult to load. Yoked together to prevent fighting or straying, their loads had to be accurately balanced to prevent loss or chafing, and required unloading every evening, only to be reloaded every morning. In some rockier parts of the desert, they were used to pull carts, but much of the terrain was too soft for wheeled vehicles. Though later travellers like Sir Aurel Stein, writing in the early years of the twentieth century, and even Charles Blackmore in 1993, described the difficulties of dealing with bad-tempered and impatient camels, the Polos, perhaps well-provided with servants and camel-drivers, and unaccustomed to any other, easier forms of transport, never complained. Aurel Stein's camels, apart from being difficult to load and exhibiting a tendency to disappear overnight, also suffered from a 'fatal inertia' which caused many losses.[9] Another native animal, the argoli or wild sheep, was named after Marco Polo. Hagenbeck attempted to bring sixty back to Russia to breed them, but they all died of diarrhoea *en route.*

Lightly loaded, bearing only jewels, which were widely accepted for trade and easy to carry, the elder Polos trekked along the northern silk route towards the Mongol capital of Karakorum. In the Desert of Lop, provided with a month's provisions, digging for brackish water every night for the camels, the Polos were subject to extra terrors beyond the physical difficulties. Travellers' legends tell of spirit voices at night which suggested bands of armed robbers, luring travellers into flight and death in the desert. The lack of navigational aids in the desert, 'nothing to guide them but the bones of men and beasts and the droppings of camels',[10] and the unvaried terrain, meant that before they tried to sleep, with the howling spirit voices filling their ears, travellers would set up a sign to show them the direction in which they should travel next day. If the sun was obscured by cloud or dust, there would be no possibility of orientation.

Temperatures ranged between the extreme heat of the day and freezing nights and, aside from siren voices, in many places there was the real danger of attack from brigands or lions. Dust storms blew up suddenly, darkening the sky, hiding the sun and compelling camel trains to stop and huddle together, trying to keep the all-pervasive dust from their eyes, noses and mouths. Today's motor vehicles are equally endangered by dust and sand storms, for the grit gets into engines and petrol, causing breakdowns. Such are the distances between settlements that even on tarmac roads, lorries travel in convoy so that drivers can help each other in the event of breakdown.

Travelling northwards towards the snow-capped Altai mountains, into the green grasslands of Mongolia, Niccolo and Maffeo Polo eventually reached the capital of Mongolia, Karakorum. They were amongst the first foreigners to visit Karakorum of their own accord, although they had been forced far to the east, away from home, by Mongol wars. They found themselves amongst the terrifying horsemen who had razed Belgrade and whose reputation was so awesome that, not long before the senior Polos set out, the mere rumour of their westward march had ruined the herring market on Britain's east coast. (Normally the Baltic fleet arrived punctually but the fear that the Mongols would proceed beyond Vienna in 1241 was such that the Baltic fleet stayed at home, leaving a rotting glut of fish in Great Yarmouth.[11]) The Polos found the city of Karakorum to be part walled city, with a great palace at its centre, and part tented encampment, reflecting the Mongols' ambivalence towards a settled life. Though the great walled palace of the Khans included a solid palace building, apartments and numerous storehouses, there was also a ceremonial tent (called *ger* in Mongol but known in the West as a *yurt*, from the Turkish) erected for the Khan in the north-eastern corner of the enclosure so that he could relive his nomadic past. Even after the construction of this permanent city, like their subjects who looked for different seasonal grazing lands, the Mongol Khans travelled to different encampments and summer palaces at fixed times of the year.

Niccolo and Maffeo had set out as ordinary merchants and must have reached Karakorum in the mid-1260s, perhaps a decade after William of Rubruck, the first religious envoy to reach the Mongol capital. As the Polos were free men, visitors arriving from the same direction as William of Rubruck, it is possible that the Mongol ruler, conscious of the need to create alliances against the common enemy of Islam, condescended to meet the Venetian traders. They say they talked to the Great Khan of religion, perhaps because they were following in William of Rubruck's footsteps and perhaps because trade might have seemed inappropriate to the solemn occasion.

The Khan's requests (or demands) for doctrinal experts, holy oil and papal response, were not easy to fulfil for, on their return to Europe in 1269, the elder Polos discovered that Pope Clement IV had died in 1268 and the appointment of a successor was considerably delayed. After waiting for two years in Venice for a new Pope to be elected, they gave up and obtained letters from a papal legate in Acre, in the absence of the real thing. In his version of the text, Ramusio adds the information that the papal legate who had provided the covering letter was eventually elected Pope Gregory X, but it is unclear whether the senior Polos were aware of this. It would have been galling to have waited so long and obtained a second-class religious recommendation only to discover that the writer of this second-class letter had finally attained the desired status.[12] It is likely, however, that Ramusio was writing with the benefit of hindsight.

When they left the Khan, he presented them with a gold tablet as a form of protection. Such gold tablets are discussed at confusing length by Yule.[13] It is difficult to assess how many the Polos eventually acquired, for they were said to have been offered more on their return journey. According to some texts, the final count was three, one on the first trip, two on the second,[14] though some make it five.[15] Strips of gold inscribed in Mongol, these were *laisser-passers* whose function recalled the proud demands in old British passports where everyone is requested and required to allow the bearer to travel freely without hindrance. Although Yule complicated his description by mentioning that the Jin used such tablets as badges of office and status, under the Liao dynasty (927–1125) they were carried by official messengers who were thereby empowered to seize horses in order to get the imperial messages through. The inscribed text of excavated Mongol tablets read, 'By the strength of the eternal heaven! May the name of the Khan be holy! Who pays him not reverence is to be slain and must die!'[16] Yule includes illustrations of some of these tablets, excavated in Russia.

Unfortunately those excavated in Russia thus far have all been silver, though Yule, in support of the Polos took 'the liberty to represent the tablet as of gold'. The number of the tablets is important, however, for in later life, back in Venice, one of them, at least, provoked a bitter argument between Marco and his uncle.

Marco was born in about 1254, six years before his father and uncle set out on their first long trip to the Far East. There has been speculation that his education was neglected during his father's long absence (between 1260 and 1270), particularly since his mother died at some time whilst her husband was away. The question of his education is usually raised in the context of his knowledge of languages, particularly the possibility that his Latin was not very good, though later he may have acquired a knowledge of Persian and

Arabic. However, it would seem that the three Polo brothers, Marco's father and his uncles, worked closely together and, indeed, eventually lived together in the Cà Polo. Thus, it is likely that Marco senior, left behind in Venice to maintain the family's trading houses and livelihood, took some interest in the education of his nephew and namesake.

When the brothers Polo embarked upon a second trip to the Far East in 1271, they took the seventeen-year-old Marco Polo with them. They were perhaps more now aware of the significance of Mongol power and, if their account of Qubilai's requests is to be believed, some faint hope of a Christian influence had been held out to them.

The second trip, across the same difficult terrain, took them to another of Qubilai Khan's great encampments, his 'summer capital' of Shangdu (or Upper Capital), Coleridge's Xanadu. The 'stately pleasure dome' was, according to Coleridge, set beside the sacred river Alph (more prosaically, the Shangdu river). Coleridge's rich imagination has the Alph sinking down through 'caverns measureless to man', which do not altogether accord with the geological foundation of the Mongol grasslands, where the poor rivers have thousands of miles to cross before they reach the sea.

The Polos found that, as at Karakorum, there were buildings of great solidity, constructed from white marble, richly gilded and fit for a universal ruler, but also wonderfully ornamented tents, elaborate *ger* or *yurts* reminding the Mongols of their nomadic heritage. Though Qubilai's summer tent could be dismantled like any ordinary *ger*, it was supported by dragon-carved uprights and tethered with 200 ropes of fine silk. Shangdu was a political centre (for it was there that Qubilai had been proclaimed Khan) but it was also a massive pleasure garden, devoted to the pursuits of hunting and falconry. Inside the huge enclosure were pine plantations – Coleridge's 'forests ancient as the hills' – and springs and streams, or 'sinuous rills', stocked with all types of deer, which the Khan sometimes hunted with leopards. Swans, cranes, pheasant and partridges abounded in the neighbourhood, fattened with millet during the hard winters and hunted with falcons.

Like the Mongol empire itself, Shangdu has disappeared, the only trace of the great palace being fragmentary stones carved in the Chinese style.[17] Qubilai's *ger* was rolled up and moved on hundreds of years ago. Even when the Polos were supposedly with him, the Khan moved all his entourage southwards in November, to his newly built capital, Khanbalik or Peking, for Shangdu was abandoned every year at the end of autumn.

14

Was it China?

According to the *Description of the World* the three Italians travelled southwards following the Khan's court into China, to 'Seres', the land of silk, which lay to the eastern edge of the world; and here they were truly pioneering European travellers.

The new ruler of China, Qubilai Khan, impressed the Polos enormously. In the *Description of the World*, he is described as 'neither short nor tall', 'well-fleshed' with his limbs in 'moderate proportion'. 'His complexion is fair and ruddy like the rose, the eyes black and handsome, the nose shapely and set squarely in place' (thank heavens it did not move about).[1] Like many later travellers to China, Marco Polo described concubinage in great detail. Each of Qubilai's four official wives had an entourage of 10,000 including beautiful maidservants and eunuchs. For his concubines, Qubilai appeared to favour women from a Mongol town called Kungurat and sent emissaries to select 400 or 500 beautiful girls every two years. Unless girls were sent in from the surrounding areas, this must have represented a considerable run on the women of Kungarat, but we are assured that it was all considered a great honour. The Khan's 'valuers' examined all the girls in great detail, peering closely at 'every feature' and awarding marks for overall beauty on a score of one to twenty or more. All those with a score of twenty or higher were brought to Qubilai, who had them reassessed, and some thirty or forty were eventually selected. They were then re-examined to make sure they were virgins and had sweet breath and didn't snore, before being divided into groups of six, who served for three days and nights until relieved by the next six. Those who had passed the last exams but were found to snore were kept in the palace and taught useful arts like glove-making 'and other elegant accomplishments' of a Victorian nature before being offered to noblemen looking for wives. Despite the detail of this description, caution must be exercised for it appears only in the late version published by Ramusio.[2]

The Khan's guards, like his women, served for three days but in groups of 3,000. There were 12,000 in all, employed, so Marco Polo says, 'not out of fear' but as a demonstration of power.[3] The 9,000 off-duty guards also stayed in the palace by day, returning home at night and only allowed to leave Peking, with permission, if a father or brother was dying.

The great banquets held by Qubilai Khan seem to have been based partly on Chinese custom, partly on Mongol practice. The Khan faced south, on a dais, raised above all those of lower rank. Music was played every time the Khan drank, and jugglers and acrobats performed after the feast. The Khan himself was served by specially chosen attendants who wore silk masks so as not to breathe on his food, which was served in gold and silver vessels. Alcohol was dispensed from a special container carved in animal forms which incorporated separate containers, each filled with different wines, including *kumis* or fermented mare's milk.[4]

Aside from jugglers, entertainment appears to have been offered in the form of punishment meted out to guests who tripped over the door. Chinese buildings invariably have a high plank beneath the door, which visitors must step over. In low, domestic buildings, it helps to keep the rain and chickens out of the house, but in the grand palace buildings, this 'threshold' was at least thirty centimetres high, some say so that those coming into the presence of the ruler were disadvantaged by the need to gather up their long robes and negotiate the obstacle, forcing them into a position of obeisance. During Qubilai Khan's banquets, huge guards with massive staves were stationed by the door, for any guest who accidentally touched the threshold as he entered was considered to have brought bad luck. He was either severely beaten or else had his clothes removed (and only returned on payment of a fine).

Hunting parties involved the employment of 10,000 men leading mastiffs or hounds. Leopards, lynxes and lions were also used to bring down wolves, foxes, fallow and roe deer, or quails. The falcons appear, like the Polos, to have travelled with the Khan (10,000 falconers with 5,000 falcons and peregrine falcons and goshawks for riverside pursuit). As he moved north, massive tents were set up en route so that the Khan could watch wildlife destruction on a grand scale from the comfort of his cushions and sable-skin rugs.[5]

The Khan's power was also evident in the number of gifts he received throughout the year. At the lunar New Year, gold, silver, pearls, bolts of fine white cloth and 100,000 white horses appeared, delivered in a procession of elephants and camels, and on his birthday, robes of beaten gold adorned with pearls and precious stones were exchanged. For the Polos, this was the supreme ruler, whose women, falcons and pearls were to be counted in millions, but he came from a family that had risen from the most abject poverty to control of most of Asia.

Like his contemporaries, Marco Polo was greatly impressed by the military power of the Mongols. He described many of their more famous battles, like the reprisal against Burma (1277), when the Muslim general of the Mongol army, Nasir al-Dīn, aware that he was outnumbered, ordered his archers to fire on the two thousand

Burmese war elephants, covering them with arrows and causing a frenzied stampede.[6] Another was the great battle in which Qubilai, taken to the battlefield on a palanquin in the form of a wooden tower carried on the back of four elephants, defeated his uncle Nayan in 1287. The battle, described out of chronological sequence, for it precedes the personal description of Qubilai (made presumably in the early 1270s), was violent, with arrows falling from the sky like rain and horses and horsemen toppling to the ground with thunderous crashes. It ended with the capture of Nayan and his slow death, wrapped in a carpet and dragged about by galloping horsemen, in a macabre version of the Mongol form of polo, where a sheep's body is fought over by cavalrymen.

Overwhelmed by the banquets, official audiences, hunting parties, and thousands of guards and palace servants, the Polos appear not to have done any trading during the years they spent in China. Apart from his travels on the Khan's business, Marco Polo is said to have stated that he spent three years as Governor of Yangzhou. However, as this claim is not corroborated in Chinese sources Paul Pelliot suggests that Polo was, perhaps, an official in the Salt Administration. Pelliot makes this suggestion partly because a person named in the official history of the Yuan (*Yuan shi*) as Polo or Boluo is listed as Salt Administrator of Yangzhou, and partly because there are so many mentions of salt manufacture and taxation in the *Description of the World*. Its production from wells, saline earth and sea pans is mentioned in areas as distant as Yunnan, Shandong and the coast of Zhejiang, although Marco Polo's Yunnanese reference may perhaps be to the Zigong area in the neighbouring province of Sichuan, where for many centuries the rock salt was drawn up from underground wells by wheels moved by water-buffaloes.[7] While this is one possible explanation, mention of salt and its significance in China is not surprising, for salt was a government-controlled product, closely linked to the new paper money.

From the Han dynasty (206 BC to AD 220) onward, salt was a state-controlled commodity and through the succeeding centuries was a taxable product, as noted in the *Description of the World*.[8] (Marco Polo mentioned it as a form of currency in Tibet.[9]) During the Song dynasty (960–1279) salt, produced as a government monopoly, was the basis upon which the new paper money was issued. Merchants could exchange paper notes, which were easy to transport, for tea or salt in the capital or at source.[10] Workers in the salt-pans of Zhejiang province were paid very little by the government and lived, in effect, in semi-slavery. However, despite the frequent references to salt, which would have been of interest to any travelling merchant or student of administration, it is difficult to find corroboration in Chinese sources of any connection between the salt administration and Marco Polo.

In fact from the Prologue to the *Description of the World*, it would appear that Marco Polo would have had little time for salt administration, since he spent the great part of his time travelling enormous distances on the Khan's business. He states that he reported as requested, but also gathered as much information as he could about places, people and customs seen *en route*, to amaze the Khan. Whether his father and uncle accompanied him on his long fact-finding missions, or sat in Peking twiddling their thumbs, is not clarified.

After seventeen years spent in China, the Polos state that they had to persuade the Khan to let them return home. Instead of returning the way they had come, a route which should have been fairly familiar to the elder Polos as they had apparently traversed it three times, they travelled home by the longest possible route, mainly by sea. According to the Prologue, Marco Polo, clearly an indefatigable traveller, had just returned from India but seemed willing to retrace his steps. As noted earlier, they were said to have accompanied a young Mongol princess, sent as a second wife to Arghun, 'lord of the Levant'.[11] Of a party of 600 which spent some eighteen months at sea, calling in at Java, Ceylon and India, 582 perished, and when they reached Arghun's court, he, too, had died. It was perhaps this brief account of mortality that led Ramusio to describe the Polos' return to Venice clad in rags and quite without luggage. In 1295 they finally returned home.

Not long after his return to Venice, Marco Polo seems to have leapt to the defence of the city (or have been called up) and ended up imprisoned after a sea battle with the Genoese. The earliest account of Marco's imprisonment and the creation of the text is given by Jacopo da Acqui. In a thirteenth-century manuscript of his *Imago Mundi* in the Biblioteca Ambrosiana, he stated that Marco Polo was taken to Genoa as a prisoner after a sea battle at Ayas between the Genoese and Venetians in 1296,[12] but even this seemingly simple statement holds contradictions. As the battle of Ayas or Laias took place in 1294, a year before the return of the Polos from Asia, da Acqui's account is generally questioned.[13] Alternatively, Ramusio's late version described Marco Polo as having rushed to the defence of Venice against the Genoese and as having been taken prisoner during the battle of Korčula (Curzola) on the Dalmatian coast on 7–8 September 1298. This date worries other authorities since the date of creation of the text is given as 1298 in the Prologue to the *Description of the World*,[14] and as prisoners from Curzola were released in 1299, some think that there would not have been enough time to create the book. If Jacques Heers' proposition is correct and Marco Polo and Rustichello were held under 'house arrest' rather than in a rat-filled dungeon, the time element is not so significant. However, as with so many other aspects of the book, it is necessary to retreat into vagueness: as Moule concluded, 'We may then think that Marco was taken pris-

oner in some obscure and otherwise unrecorded engage-
ment of armed merchantmen in 1296 . . .'.[15]

One of the most important family events after the return
of the travellers in 1295 was the purchase by Niccolo and
Maffeo of a house in Venice in the San Giovanni Grisostomo
district, apparently some time in the 1290s.[16] Ramusio's
romantic tale of the return of the foreign-looking travellers
forms part of the legend of Marco Polo and it would be
churlish to interrupt it to point out that the house to which
Ramusio says they returned would have been far from wel-
coming as the Polo family did not buy it for another few
years.[17] It is not clear from surviving documents whether or
not Marco Polo was involved in this purchase although the
site of the house is still known as Cà (house) Milion or
Corte del Milion, tying it particularly to Marco Polo, who
was known as '*il milione*', or as the Cà Polo. The house was
situated on a corner where the Rio di San Giovanni Grisostomo meets the Rio di San Marina. In the summer of 1596,
the house was destroyed by fire (and the prompt service
of the firemen rewarded with six ducats each from the
Senate).[18] In 1677, the site, 'commonly called Camilion and
partly vacant', was sold so that a theatre could be built there,
the Teatro Malibran. Surviving near the original site is a
tower with Byzantine arches (though this probably never
formed part of the Cà Polo) but nothing else remains.

Despite the production of the book which was, eventually,
to make him a household name throughout the world,
Marco and the other Polos were never offered any official
recognition or status by the city of Venice, either as merchants or travellers. As merchants of no particular status,
the few surviving documents relating to their trading activities are mainly legal documents, attesting to mercantile
activity only where it went wrong. Some time after his return
from China, Marco Polo apparently sued his agent for non-
payment on a pound and a half of musk.[19] Another document in the Venetian archives, dated 1305, concerns wine

smuggling by Bonocio of Mestre, one of whose guarantors was Marco Polo.[20] This latter document is of particular interest since Marco Polo is named as '*marcus paulo milion*', the first reference to the appellation '*il milione*'.

Marco Polo died in 1324, leaving a will, and three daughters, Fantina, Bellela and Moreta. The will, drawn up shortly before his death,[21] makes no mention of properties overseas (as his uncle's will did) or travel. The major evidence of contact with the East is the grant of his freedom and a small legacy to Peter, his 'Tartar slave' (*petrum famulum meum de genere tartarorum*),[22] whose own will was registered in 1329, where he is described as Petrus Suliman.[23] It is generally assumed that he had been brought back from the Far East by Marco Polo, but the combination of names, Peter and Suliman, Christian and Muslim, and the appellation 'Tartar' are confusing.

The medieval chronicler Matthew Paris used Tartar to mean Mongol[24] and it seems to have been generally used by 'outsiders' to refer to Mongols long after Qinghis Khan had virtually eliminated the Mongol Tartar tribe.[25] If he was a Mongol of some sort, the most likely group would be either the Mongols of Persia, who had fully adopted Islam by 1295 (a bit late for this narrative), or those of the 'Golden Horde' on the Volga, rather than the Chinese-based Mongols who, though tolerant of Islam, were more Buddhist than anything else.[26] The *Description of the World* contains several mentions of Tartars converting to Islam and notes this difference with China: 'Those who live in Cathay have adopted the manners and customs of the idolators . . . while those who live in the Levant have adopted the manners of the Saracens.'[27] It may be that Polo used 'Tartar' very loosely to indicate anything to the east of Jerusalem, and Petrus Suliman's surname may be more significant, placing him within the Islamic world. The Christian appellation 'Petrus' or Peter may have been given for convenience, perhaps to replace a more complicated foreign name. As he and his wife seem to have lived with the Polo family until his death, other less-travelled members of the family might have found a familiar name easier to remember and pronounce. Petrus could have been acquired anywhere (and he does not appear in the *Description of the World*, either by name or inference).

There is equally little to connect Marco Polo directly with China in the detailed inventory of his possessions at the time of his death, a document which was drawn up in 1366, considerably afterwards, as a result of a quarrel between Marco's recently widowed elder daughter Fantina and her husband's family.[28] The list comprised over 200 entries, including a bag of rhubarb (a remedy for constipation),[29] which was described (accurately) in the *Description of the World* as growing in the Gansu area and being exported all over the world.[30] The importance of Gansu rhubarb to the Western digestion was absorbed into Chinese folklore, for when Opium Commissioner Lin Zexu wrote to Queen Victoria in August 1839 requesting her to stop the opium trade, he included a threat to prevent the export of Chinese rhubarb to the United Kingdom in the certain hope that it would bring the constipated country to its knees.[31] As it is listed as a possession of Marco Polo's at his death in 1324, it is just possible that he had acquired it early on his travels, when he mentioned the country of Tangut, and carried it with him throughout his journey, so that it would have been indeed a bag of almost one hundred-year-old Chinese rhubarb. However, as it was an established medicine (though William of Rubruck claimed it nearly killed a friend of his), it could equally have been a more recent purchase, imported by one of the merchants he had dealings with later in life.

In addition to the rhubarb, there were twenty-four beds, endless pairs of sheets (many of silk), fabrics such as '*lino laurado con seda*' (linen embroidered with silk), silk embroidered with gold or decorated with '*stranij animali*' (or fabulous animals), three gold rings, coats, pieces of wool and cooking pots. Much of the silk listed, when not plain and white for sheeting, sounds from the brief descriptions to be very much in the Persian or Near Eastern style, embroidered and worked with gold thread, and far more opulent and heavier than Chinese silks.

The list records reasonable and practical, if not sumptuous, possessions, and in few cases offers evidence of direct contact with China. Moule suggests that one item can be read either as a 'piece of cloth of gold made to order', which would be of Near-Eastern rather than Chinese origin, or *'tables d'or des comandemens'*, which would be the sort of passport or permission to travel inscribed on gold of the type handed to his father and uncle when they left Karakorum to return home after their first trip. A gold *laisser-passer* or passport of this type was the subject of a dispute between Marco and his uncle Maffeo. In Maffeo's will of 1310 there is a passage relating to the still unresolved question of a loan to Marco of money, jewels and a gold tablet from the Great Khan. The money in question was apparently repayment for a loss incurred in Trebizong (Trabzon). There is no date given for this loss so it is impossible to tell whether it was incurred through normal trading activities or on their famous travels.[32] Marco's possible possession of a golden tablet and evidence of an argument with his uncle of sufficient gravity to be recorded in his will suggest considerable family division. In Marco's defence, it could be argued that there appear to have been several of these handed out, to his father and uncle, at least, on different occasions and if he was, as he claimed, with them, he might have been entitled to one. The inventory of his possessions is partly illegible and appears, if it refers to a gold tablet at all, to use a different term for it than that which appears in his uncle's will.[33]

Though the scanty evidence we have for Marco Polo's activities in Venice suggests only that he continued to be involved with mercantile matters, the view of one of his contemporaries, Friar Pipino of Bologna, who translated the *Description of the World* into Latin during Marco Polo's lifetime, was that it was not the materialistic and mercantile, but the religious aspect of the book that was most important, revealing the wonders of Creation and contrasting the dark pagan world of idolators with that of Christianity. Despite this accolade, there is, unfortunately, no evidence of any papal recognition of any of the Polos and the religious aspects of their mission, just as there was no official recognition of their travels made by their home town of Venice.

15

A significant absence

Marco Polo claimed considerable intimacy with the Khan and might, therefore, have been eligible for inclusion in the voluminous Chinese documents relating to the period; yet one of the most puzzling aspects of his story, given his self-stated position of importance and closeness with the court, is the lack of a reference to the Polos in Chinese sources (or Mongol sources for that matter).[1] However, it is not only the official sources that are important, for the mysterious Novgorodian delegation of 1261 is absent from the official record, but was mentioned in a diary kept by a courtier.

There is a mass of Chinese material to be consulted, from the official history of the dynasty to the local histories (gazetteers) produced for every district, and it is difficult to follow a straight thread through the morass. When I first looked at Chinese sources, I went to the primary documents, the official histories of the period, trawling acres of paper in search of a mention of an Italian or a Polo. Later on, I came across a compendium volume of contemporary Chinese essays written in defence of Marco Polo, and there, contrary to my expectations, I found the first refutation of the often repeated claim that Marco Polo served as a governor of Yangzhou.[2] Professor Yang Zhijiu, a spirited but by no means uncritical defender of Marco Polo as the first

European traveller to China, noted that the widely repeated claim that Marco Polo governed Yangzhou was based on a misreading in one text. Where Marco Polo originally seems to have said he '*sejourna*' or 'stayed' in Yangzhou for three years, this was miscopied as '*governa*' or 'governed'. Taking this more plausible reading, no one else need plough through lists of Governors or officials in Yangzhou. This was not, however, Marco Polo's only claim to fame in China, and this one was hardly his fault, but a tantalising copyist's error.

Polo did, however, also state that he worked as an official emissary and helped to end the bloody siege of Xiangyang. Despite these claims, it has been demonstrated that he and his father and uncle could not have been instrumental in the ending of the siege of Xiangyang for it ended in 1273, before they could possibly have arrived there if they set out in 1270. Moreover, as I mentioned earlier, Chinese histories record the importation of Persian engineers to construct the siege-breaking mangonels that the Polos and their entourage were supposed to have made. When I first started ploughing through Chinese sources for evidence of his official service, I therefore concentrated on his claim to have been entrusted 'with all the most interesting and distant missions' by the Khan and (before reading Professor Yang) to have 'governed' Yangzhou 'for three years'.

As for his service as a travelling reporter for Qubilai, there is no record anywhere of such service. Though the level of intimacy he claims with the Khan would suggest that he should have deserved a mention in the official records, along with Persian siege-breakers and Indian doctors, it is possible that he was not quite as important as he claimed. It is not inconceivable that Qubilai could have been interested in the curious customs and habits of the Chinese people he was currently conquering and that another 'foreigner' might have been similarly more interested in such anthropological detail than a courtier. If Marco Polo was less important than he claimed, it is difficult to imagine him travelling about China for seventeen years on official missions. If he was as important as he claimed, his omission from the records remains puzzling.

Local gazetteers were produced for all the major towns and districts in China, in another example of the massive bureaucracy which recorded all sorts of details of local administration, agricultural produce, industrial manufacture, local notables (including virtuous widows) and events of significance, Their periodic appearance indicates that they were continually up-dated, and they all contain significant chunks of local history. Even if Polo was a sojourner in Yangzhou, rather than a governor, it is likely that a visitor of exotic foreign origin would have been included. Indeed, trawling these gazetteers and related works like the *Yangzhou tujing*, a late eighteenth-century work on the town which lists notables by dynasty, it is fascinating to see the strange, non-Chinese names of Mongol officials appointed during the Yuan dynasty (1279–1368). These appear suddenly amongst the very restricted number of Chinese surnames that occur over and over again.

There are a limited number of surnames in China, whose people traditionally refer to themselves as the 'old hundred names'. Of these 'hundred', only a relatively small number are dominant. Amongst the Lis, Wangs, Zhangs and Tangs, virtually all followed by a two-character 'given name', the sudden appearance of peculiar characters like 'Bo' and 'A', which are not part of the list of the hundred surnames, is very striking. They are also often listed in four-character combinations, quite unlike the normal three-character name composed of surname and double-character given name, Mao Zedong, Deng Xiaoping, Zhou Enlai and so on. There are a very small number of 'double-barrelled' surnames in China, such as Ouyang and Situ and Sima, but these are well-known: in general the four-character groupings with 'surnames' created from very unusual characters immediately mark their owners as non-Chinese. Yet Polo's name does not appear in these texts, nor is his tenure mentioned in the Yangzhou *difangzhi,* or gazetteers, of which editions produced in 1542, 1601, 1685, 1819, 1874 and 1947 survive.

Similarly, in the *Yuan shi,* produced along the same lines as all the previous dynastic histories since the Han (206 BC–AD 220) on the basis of officially created archives, there is a mass of strange names. The index to the twenty-four dynastic histories[3] lists a number of people called Boluo, which can get excitingly close to the Italians, as in the old English romanisation system (Wade–Giles) it was rendered 'Polo'.

As early as 1865, Gaston Pauthier decided that he had found a reference to Marco Polo in one of these 'Polo' entries. One Polo (or Boluo or Poluo as the current *pinyin* romanisation has it, depending upon which characters are used) was mentioned in the *Yuan shi* as serving as vice-president of the Secret Council and Governor of the province of Yunnan and, in 1284, as superintendent of the Salt Administration centred on Yangzhou itself.[4] Unfortunately, despite the initial excitement, painstaking Professor Pelliot demonstrated that it was apparent from both this text and references in Rashid al-Dīn that the person in question was in fact a Mongol, named Poulad by Rashid and Bolod aqa in the Mongol.[5] The Boluo, Poluo or Polo name is simply a transliteration of the sound of the Mongol. (The characters themselves have no meaning and are used only for their sound values, though 'bo' or 'po' can mean 'a sprouting plant', 'a shooting star' or, in Matthews' dictionary, 'to pop glutinous rice in a pan', and 'luo', or 'lo', means 'a net' or 'to spread out'.)[6]

Of the twenty-one Boluos or Polos in the index to the twenty-four dynastic histories, virtually all occur in the histories of non-Chinese dynasties: fifteen in the Yuan or Mongol history and four in the dynastic history of the Jin

(1115–1234), another non-Chinese northern group; so it is evident that the connotations are Mongol and northern. Trying another sound character used to romanise non-Chinese names in Chinese history, Bu (or Pu), which means 'no' when it is not being used for its sound alone, is found in eleven instances, six occurring in the Yuan history, one in the Jin history and two very early (in the Later Han dynasty and the *Shi Ji* or universal history compiled in the second century BC), but never in conjunction with any 'lo' or 'luo' sounds.

Leonardo Olschki, who noted another Mongol Polo or Boluo (executed in 1330 for black magic and sacrifices to the Great Bear), suggested that it was wrong to look for the Polos under a version of their surname.[7] He proposed that the Polos' 'visiting cards' would have stressed their Christian names, with Marco as Mojuci (Mo-chu-tzu in Wade–Giles), Niccolo as Niegula (or Nie-ku-la) and Maffeo using a form that was used from the sixteenth century to transcribe St Matthew the Apostle's name, 'mingtai' (ming-t'ai in Wade–Giles), possibly appending Baolu (or Pao-lu) as a surname, again based on the translation of St Paul's name. But these forms, whilst perhaps medievally correct, do not appear in the dynastic histories, either.[8]

In the absence of individual reference, Franke examined the *Yuan shi* for references to Europeans, and discovered mention of Alans, Qypcaa, Russians and Bulgarians (Puliaer). The Chinese and Mongols were often as vague about the exact origin of 'foreigners' as were their European contemporaries about different Mongol tribes, so these references could possibly be stretched to cover Italians; but as they date from 1330 and 1332 they are all later than the Polos' supposed visit.[9] Rashīd al-Dīn was equally vague, even when writing about the 'Franks' in his World History, and omitted all mention of Italians.[10]

Nevertheless, for the Chinese today, Marco Polo is a figure of great significance. He brought China to the attention of fourteenth-century Europe, the first westerner to write about China, apparently from his own experience. As the preface to Yu Shixiong's book states, 'Marco Polo is an international figure. He was born in Italy but his most important activities took place in China. His book is a contribution to world culture, loved and studied by the people of the world, a rare treasure shared by the people of the world.'

The *Description of the World* was first translated into Chinese in 1913 and, like the rest of the world, its readers accepted the story it told. In 1941, Professor Yang Zhijiu discovered, in section 19418 of the *Yongle dadian* (*Great Compendium of the Yongle period*, a manuscript encyclopaedia in 22,937 sections compiled between 1403 and 1408 and bound in 11,095 volumes), the description of the voyage of the Mongol princess sent to marry Arghun, Ilkhān of Persia, in 1292. His work was used by Francis Woodman Cleaves, for it appeared to corroborate Marco Polo's description of how the Polos made their way home.[11] Sources like this at first appear to confirm Marco Polo's presence in China, but though the *Yongle dadian* version does generally tally with Marco Polo's account, it unfortunately contains no reference to the Polos or to any Italians at all. Cleaves' Persian source similarly failed to mention any Italians. Cleaves dismissed the lack of names by pointing out that the princess herself is never mentioned by name in the *Yongle dadian*. Nevertheless, it is difficult not to conclude that whilst the princess' voyage did take place, this is another example of Marco Polo's retelling of a well-known tale (like the invasion of Japan or Wang Zhu's uprising). If he and his relatives were, indeed, part of the entourage, they must have been of insignificant rank, unworthy of individual note.

Professor Yang, the pre-eminent Chinese defender of Marco Polo, admitted that his discovery does not actually refer to Marco Polo, but went on to state that official court records were not in the habit of listing such characters. Continuing his defence of Marco Polo's veracity (though admitting that he exaggerated because he did not have a very good education and was not an historian), it was Professor Yang who first defended the. omission of tea by suggesting that Marco Polo perhaps kept up his Italian habits and did not drink it; and, since the Mongols 'were not great tea-drinkers' and Marco Polo kept company with them rather than with Chinese people, it was of no interest to him.[12] Professor Yang noted further that an American academic had argued with scholarship and detail that Marco Polo might only have reached Peking and written about China from what he had heard there.[13] This argument appeared acceptable to Professor Yang, as an argument, though to me it raises the question of how the Polos supported themselves and what they did for seventeen years if Marco, at least, was not busy and gainfully employed as a messenger.

Professor Yang also refuted the German Mongolists' arguments: considering, for example, that omissions such as tea and the Great Wall were not sufficient to dismiss the whole book, and stressing that the use of Persian vocabulary was due to the Mongols' use of Persian and Turkish advisors. In the light of his strong defence of Marco Polo, Professor Yang was distressed by the fact that, in contrast with the Americans, contemporary British scholars were turning their back on the pro-Polo scholarship of the nineteenth century, exemplified by the tortuous efforts of Sir Henry Yule,[14] and called for British scholars to return to Yule's fold.

In his essay, he did not address himself to the omission of foot-binding, although he could have done so by stressing, once again, Marco Polo's separateness from the Chinese (as opposed to the large-footed Mongols). That he did not raise this matter is no doubt due largely to the fact that the contemporary Chinese are horrified by the ancient practice and consider Western interest in it an insult. There are very few old ladies still alive whose feet were bound early this century, although in the early 1980s you could still find specialist sections in shoe shops in Peking where two sizes of tiny black corduroy shoes were sold for those with bound feet. No doubt for all the wrong reasons (an unhealthy interest in the feudal past or unconscious foot-fetishism), I always longed to buy a pair but did not dare, as I was too well aware that it would have been considered insulting to modern China.

Though I was very impressed by the research of Chinese scholars, especially Professor Yang's discovery about the return voyage, it still seemed to me that, despite the care with which they championed Marco Polo as an early friend of China, their research still did not demonstrate that Marco Polo actually stayed in China, only that some of his stories tally with events, and he remains a significant absence in the mass of documentation on the Mongol period.

Conclusions

Beginning with the negative, the *Description of the World* is not an itinerary or a straightforward account of travels. Experienced travellers attempting to follow in Marco Polo's footsteps were invariably forced to abandon the attempt: John Julius Norwich admitted to having to give up following the trail somewhere in Persia; Lord Macartney's embassy was forced into geographical hypothesis round and about the Great Wall; and Clarence Dalrymple Bruce became deeply confused in the Persian Gulf.[1]

If it is not an itinerary (excepting the Prologue with its sparse details), the rest of the text fulfils more accurately the promise of the title as a 'description of the world' beyond Venice. One of the spurs to its compilation may have been the slightly premature sense that there was a growing demand for geographies in the late thirteenth and early fourteenth centuries. Jacopo da Acqui, Vincent of Beauvais and even Sir John Mandeville all compiled world histories and geographies, an activity paralleled by Rashīd al-Dīn in his *World History* in Arabic. The appearance of these early geographies heralded the great age of discovery when pioneering seafarers set out to prove the limits of written description. Christopher Columbus had a copy of Polo's *Description of the World* with him on his epic voyage, though the fact that he ended up on the other side of the world was not due solely to the difficulty of physically following in Polo's footsteps. Unaware of the American land mass that lay in the way, he had convinced himself that he could get to Asia by sailing westwards and found himself making topographical somersaults trying to identify Cuba with Japan (where Marco Polo only described a palace and a major sea-battle fought two hundred years previously). Christopher Columbus' own copy of Marco Polo with marginal notes still survives in the Capitular and Columbus Library of Seville,[2] but his scribbles do not appear to hint at massive disillusion.

The gradual growth in popularity of the genre of travel writing is evident in the translation and spread of manuscript editions of the *Description of the World*. Some fifty years later, Sir John Mandeville's fictional account, *Travels*, was greeted with the same enthusiasm: it, too, was translated and was available in every common European language by 1400 and Czech, Danish, Dutch and Irish by 1500.[3] It is perhaps significant that some of the early copies of the *Description of the World* were reproduced as part of collections of works of travel and topography, which also often included Sir John Mandeville's *Travels*.

The *Travels* also formed part of Christopher Columbus' pre-exploration researches,[4] but by comparison it is interesting that, not long after Ramusio rediscovered and promoted Marco Polo as a great traveller, doubts began to be expressed about Mandeville's veracity. By the early sixteenth century, Bishop Joseph Hall was referring to the 'whetstone leasings of old Mandeville', and a satirical play of 1636, *The Antipodes*, by Richard Brome, was based entirely on Mandeville, who by that time must have been almost a household name, albeit as a fake.[5] It has been demonstrated that Mandeville did, in fact, lift passages from fifteen or more sources, including Vincent de Beauvais and Odoric of Pordenone,[6] his word-by-word copying giving the lie to his claims. In contrast, the second-hand nature of the *Description of the World*, written by

Rustichello from information provided by Marco Polo and added to by later translators, may have helped to conceal any obvious borrowings. As Mandeville's star waned, Marco Polo was enjoying a posthumous revival which still flourishes.

It is possible that the lack of a coherent itinerary in Marco Polo's *Description of the World* may be due to the enthusiasm of the romance-writer Rustichello, who could have dictated the form of the text and encouraged its expansion beyond a description of travel into a grander world history with the incorporation of irrelevant geographical descriptions of places like Russia and Japan and ancient battles.

It was perhaps Rustichello, a writer by profession, who hoped to exploit the growing popular demand for such books on the marvels of the distant corners of the world. The method of creation of the text is probably crucial. Though we do not know for sure even which battle it was that resulted in Marco Polo's imprisonment, one of the relative certainties about the *Description of the World* is that it was written as a joint effort. Impressed by the fantastic tales told by Marco Polo to pass the time, whether in a dungeon or other form of confinement, Rustichello perhaps proposed a literary collaboration. In the days before printing and copyright, it is difficult to imagine making a fortune out of a best-circulating (rather than best-selling) manuscript; but Rustichello, who had previously relied upon the support of the heir to the English throne as a result of his literary efforts, may have aimed for similar favour.

The source material that they used to create the work is more difficult. If Marco Polo arrived back in Venice in only the clothes he stood up in (albeit with jewels sewn into their linings) as Jacopo da Acqui described, he is unlikely to have had many personal papers, which Jacopo da Acqui also described as being sent for from prison. If family, rather than personal, papers were provided, they might well have included material relating to family trading trips eastwards and, perhaps, Persian guidebooks for merchants. There may have been Persian historical works which enabled them to include ancient battles, and descriptions of Russia and Japan that were not part of Marco Polo's or his family's personal experience.

Yule noted that the earliest foreign eyewitness descriptions of China were 'all, with one slight exception, Arabic'.[7] The Arabic accounts of China, written from the Tang dynasty onwards, were based on close contact, for Arabic and Persian traders, attracted by rich produce and exotic culture, resided in the major cities and ports of China most involved in the export of porcelain and silks, such as Chang'an (the capital, today's Xi'an), Canton, Quanzhou and Fuzhou. Paul Pelliot's work on Marco Polo's vocabulary (or that of his multitudinous copyists) contains much reference to Persian and Arabic sources. Examination of Arabic and Persian sources was also considered to be of paramount importance by Herbert Franke, not only for the vain hope that there might be a reference to Marco Polo, but also for the possibility that Marco Polo might have relied upon a Persian guidebook as his major source material.[8]

An anonymous Arab writing in 851[9] described the port of Canton and its mosque, public granaries and dispensaries, the complex administration and its stress on the written document, the practice of secondary burial, protection afforded to travellers, and the use of porcelain, rice-wine and tea. Other Arab travellers to China in the Tang dynasty have left similarly detailed accounts, but it is the later accounts, including the *World History* of Rashīd al-Dīn, and Ibn Baṭṭūṭa's early fourteenth-century account of his travels, which provide the closest parallels to parts of the *Description of the World*.

Rashīd al-Dīn, the most significant writer in the Marco Polo story, was a Jew, the son of an apothecary, born in about 1247 in Hamadan. He converted to Islam at the age of thirty. He seems to have entered the service of Abaqa (ruled 1265–82), the second Mongol Khan of Persia, as a physician. His great achievement was the compilation of a universal history of the world, undertaken at the order of Öljeitü (Khan of Persia, ruled 1304–16). His *Jāmi 'al-Tawārīkh* (*Complete collection of histories*) included a history of the Franks (Europeans) and a history of China from the earliest creation legends to the reign of Temür Öljeitü, Qubilai's successor (ruled 1294–1307).

Rashīd's history of China in many instances paralleled Marco Polo's account. As Professor Pelliot demonstrated, the spelling of place-names frequently tallied, though it is obviously less surprising to find Persian versions in Rashīd. Even where there are mysteries or mistakes, such as the exact location of Iachi (the 'Duck' pond or 'Ear' Lake) in Yunnan, Rashīd and Polo run parallel. Their accounts of the murder of Wang Zhu are equally and similarly confused.

Rashīd was writing an account of China which was not personal, for he did not visit the country, but relied instead on various contemporary sources, both written and verbal, and, as *Encyclopaedia Britannica* has it, his sources were Mongol. For his history of the Mongols, he used the *Golden Book*, a chronicle of Mongol history, and for the campaigns of Qinghis Khan, the narrative of Juwaynī (1226–83).[10] The basis for his account of China is unknown.[11] Rashid sets out Chinese history according to the traditional chronological arrangement of dynasties, beginning with the Xia (supposedly from *c.* twenty-first to sixteenth century BC) and ending early in the Mongol era. The fact that the non-Chinese Jin dynasty (which ruled North China after its capture from the the Chinese Song dynasty between 1125 and 1234) is regarded by Rashīd as 'legitimate' suggests that his source was more recent than the Song period for a 'Song author could never have listed the Jin emperors as legal rulers of China'.[12]

Another Persian author, Bernaketi, apparently stated that two Chinese assisted Rashīd in his history. Following this clue and – pace *Encyclopaedia Britannica* – hoping for a Chinese source for Rashīd's history (a parallel to the Persian source he thinks might have been used by Marco Polo), Professor Franke was excited to discover a Chinese Buddhist account by Nianchang. The *Fozu lidai tongzai* (*Account of the Buddhist ancestral generations*) described events up to 1333 and included prefaces to the printed editions dated 1341 and 1344, in which 'the parallels are so striking and so numerous' that it could well have been the source for Rashīd. Unfortunately, Rashīd's history was completed some twenty years earlier in 1310.

As the dates do not tally, if Nianchang's work was not Rashīd's source Professor Franke suggested that there must have been some (as yet undiscovered) Chinese Buddhist chronicle which served as a 'common source for Nianchang as well as for the monks who, according to Benaketi, compiled the chronicle serving as a source for Rashīd'.[13]

Ibn Baṭṭūṭa's account of China presents some of the same problems. He was a native of Tangier, born in 1304, who spent much of his life, between 1325 and 1355, travelling in the Far East. His account of his travels was apparently written down in 1355.[14] Ibn Baṭṭūṭa's description of Hangzhou included the pleasure boats and entertainers, the markets and their produce, including bamboo handicrafts, and he remarked upon the intensive cultivation of the eastern seaboard of China.[15] He also described paper money, coal and china clay, silk and its production, and the consumption of pork.[16] That Marco Polo did not single out pork, still the favoured meat of China, could be because its popularity was less striking to a Christian. Ibn Baṭṭūṭa also noted, without citing the place where they were found, enormous cocks and hens,[17] not unlike Marco Polo's giant geese.[18]

Although there are differences in emphasis, such as Polo's failure to remark upon the cultivation of the Yangtse delta area (defenders of Polo might leap forward to point out that he was a city-dweller, not a farmer), the similarities between Ibn Baṭṭūṭa's and Polo's descriptions of China are striking. It is these similarities that led Herbert Franke to suggest that Marco Polo might, perhaps, have been relying upon a Persian or Arabic guidebook to China filled with the sort of detail that both he and Ibn Baṭṭūṭa provided. Though several have searched for such a guidebook, it is unfortunate that the thirteenth century is a 'Dark Ages of Persian popular literature'[19] and no such guidebook has surfaced. Thus Franke concluded that, in the absence of any clear source, Marco Polo must be left with the benefit of the doubt.

Nevertheless, his possible reliance upon Arabic or Persian sources could explain the similarities with Rashīd and Ibn Baṭṭūṭa, particularly in vocabulary and in the odd descriptions such as the giant fowl of the south. It might also explain his padding out of his description with events that he had not seen, like the attempted invasion of Japan, early Mongol battles and the complexities of the Wang Zhu affair. If he had, indeed, been provided with documentation by his family whilst in prison, a Persian guidebook in the family's possession, or Persian accounts of the Mongol conquests, could have given him source material.

The question of Marco Polo's possible reliance upon Persian sources is very difficult to resolve since nothing that fits the bill has yet been discovered. Rashīd al-Dīn's account, which closely parallels Marco Polo in parts, appeared too late in its finished form to have been any use to him, as did Ibn Baṭṭūṭa's. Even Rashīd al-Dīn's sources, as Professor Franke has demonstrated, are tantalising. Though, given the enormous stress in China on the preservation and transmission of written texts, it is still possible that a Chinese source for parts of Rashīd al-Dīn's *World History* may be discovered.

Reliance on other people's work to fill out the *Description of the World* might account for some of the glaring omissions, for Persian and Arab travellers had a longer tradition of knowledge about the Far East and, coming from a different culture, might have been surprised by different things. For Chinese historians like Yang Zhijiu the omission of significant details, amidst all the detail that was included, is not seen as a major problem, and the argument has its points, for if Marco Polo had included everything there was in China, he and Rustichello would probably never have emerged from prison. Perhaps we should accept the editorial prerogative of author and ghost writer to miss things out. Foot-binding might interest me but not Polo and Rustichello.

Professor Yang also considered, with some reason, that getting things wrong is not necessarily a result of a reliance upon second-hand sources. The errors in the story of Wang Zhu's assassination attempt were also made by Rashīd al-Dīn, so anyone could make a mistake. Marco Polo's failure to set down the accurate lineage of Qubilai Khan, mentioned as a problem by Craig Clunas, was also dismissed by Yang as an easy mistake and, given the complexities of the various Mongol empires and their rulers, he had a point.

Some of the mistakes cannot be Marco Polo's 'fault' but are clear indications that second-hand material was used, perhaps by others. That copyists took on the role of 'improvers' and compilers seems evident from the account of the defeat of Togta by Nogai, which occurs only in the fifteenth-century Toledo version.[20] According to Rashīd, this battle occurred in 1298–99 and thus could not have been known to Marco Polo and Rustichello in time for its inclusion in the (lost) original manuscript, unless we discount the date of compilation given in the Prologue. This must be a later 'improvement' to the text, raising the question of how much 'improvement' and interpolation occurred and how early.

Yet if Marco Polo was not in China, there is, unfortunately, nothing to prove he was anywhere else.

In the absence of proof of his existence elsewhere between 1271 and 1295, there is only the *Description of the*

World for evidence, and I think that the complicated struc-ture of the book may offer some insight. The details offered in the Prologue to the *Description of the World* refer at greatest length to the early journey by Marco's father and uncle. Their plausible eastward progress from their known bases in the Crimea and Constantinople, driven on by war and chance meetings with important persons, may perhaps be the only concrete evidence of such a journey by any Polo.

The sudden transformation of his father and uncle from merchants to self-appointed papal go-betweens could have been the springboard for Marco Polo's description of a second, longer journey. The existence of the golden pass-ports are evidence of reasonably high-level contact with one of the Mongol rulers, though not necessarily Qubilai him-self. Might part of the family dispute over gold tablets (revealed in 1310, after the compilation of the *Description of the World*) have been Marco Polo's claim to have been there himself when he wasn't? Might his father and uncle have made a dangerous journey and returned with one or more gold *laisser-passer* tablets, only to have had their chance of glory stolen by Marco writing himself into the story whilst in prison? To add insult to injury, Maffeo's will of 1310 suggests some jiggery-pokery over one of these gold tablets by Marco. Different texts suggest that a varying number of these tablets were distributed to the Polos at different times; it is not easy to count how many there eventually were, and whether Marco himself ever received one from the hands of the Khan. The dispute, recorded in a will, seems perhaps more significant than the possible number surviving.

Perhaps in the final analysis the text should be treated as two separate entities. The details of the Prologue, particu-larly those describing the first trip of Niccolo and Maffeo Polo, suggest a credible venture, whilst the rest of the text is a mixture of legend and geographical and historical description which hangs together in a quite different way. I think it quite likely that the elder Polos travelled a long way across the deserts of Central Asia, like William of Rubruck and John of Plano Carpini, perhaps to Karakorum or a Mongol encampment nearby, and returned, protected by the gold safe-conduct tablets of one of the Mongol leaders. Marco's participation and the whole second trip seems unlikely, even allowing for exaggeration.

That Marco Polo himself might not have gone to Karakorum, let alone Peking, seems more likely to me than that he wrote everything he knew from a view of Peking (as John Haeger suggested). The major part of the book is a description of China and beyond. If he had spent years in Peking, a more detailed account of that city alone by its first Italian, or indeed European, visitor would have been sufficiently exotic to attract attention.

If he did not travel to China and India and the South East Asian archipelago, where did he get his information? Family stories and family familiarity with the Near East and beyond could have provided much material. His father and uncle's plausible excursion to Karakorum was a valuable starting point. Though merchant secrecy was an important aspect of safeguarding sources of supply, a family with houses in the Crimea and Constantinople might have gathered material, including Persian guidebooks, maps and histories, on the areas beyond in order to facilitate travel and trade. If Pegolotti could write a credible guide to merchant travel to China based entirely on second-hand information, Marco Polo could, too. Franke has demonstrated the difficulty of finding the Chinese source for Rashīd al-Dīn's history of China and raised the same problem as occurs in comparison between Polo and Rashīd: an uncanny similarity, but a chronological impossibility. It is equally difficult to demonstrate a reliance upon the rich sources provided by European missionaries, for William of Rubruck's report was apparently not widely circulated and Marco Polo was clearly not in a position to trawl libraries during the period of his collaboration with Rustichello.

Odoric of Pordenone's later account, which tallies with Marco Polo in parts, and yet departs from Polo in parts, could not have helped Marco Polo, but may itself have been partly based on Marco Polo's book.

The sources used by Marco Polo and Rustichello must have been information of the sort available to Rashīd al-Dīn: perhaps written sources on geography and Mongol history, and much oral legend relating to the marvels of the East, the Magis' home village, the legendary Prester John and his real 'grandson' George, salamanders, and foxes that ate only sugar-cane. Family knowledge might have been the basis for much of the information on produce such as dates and on handicrafts like pearl-piercing in Baghdad. Combined with Rustichello's flourishes and, perhaps, dictated by his sense of composition, the text remains valuable, even if not an eyewitness account.

Whilst I incline to the view that Marco Polo himself probably never travelled much further than the family's trading posts on the Black Sea and in Constantinople, and was not responsible for Italian ice-cream or Chinese dumplings, this does not mean that the *Description of the World* does not remain a valuable source of information on China and the Near East, in particular. His usefulness as a recorder of information otherwise lost is similar to the case of Herodotus (*c.* 484 BC to *c.* 425 BC), who did not travel to all the places he described and who mixed fact with fantastic tales, but whose work is nevertheless not to be discarded lightly.[21] When used in conjunction with Arabic, Persian and Chinese texts which bear out the spirit, if not always the detail, of its contents, the *Description of the World* remains a very rich source. The portrait of the chessboard city plan of Peking still stands, and remains, whatever its source, a credible account of a city which no longer exists, but which has its place in the history of the settlements in the area. The contents of the *Description of the World,,* used critically, remain important, and can be regarded as an example of the type of world geography which was beginning to become popular in the fourteenth century. This interest in the world beyond Europe and its legends, rulers and products led to the great voyages of exploration of the late fourteenth and fifteenth centuries; and even in the early twentieth century, great travellers like Sir Aurel Stein set off into the little-known Gobi desert, for which Marco Polo's *Description of the World* remained one of the few reference sources, however unreliable.

Afterword
to the
American Edition

Though I was fairly sure of my ground, I was worried about the publication of the British edition of this book. I was aware that it covered many fields and that I'd strayed well beyond my own area of study, but one of the things that I wanted to do was to stimulate discussion and not, by any means, to provide the last word. I did not want to be seen as a destroyer of myths, setting up the well-known figure of Marco Polo for the all-too-easy retrospective destruction. Rather I had hoped to provoke readers into looking for themselves at an unfamiliar mass of interesting material. I am very grateful to scholars like Professors Herbert Franke and Daniel Waley for sending me lists of corrections to improve my previous text.

Much of the discussion that followed publication revolved around the question of omissions from Marco Polo's text. I was made aware that I, too, had omitted omissions: there is no mention of chopsticks, for example, and I had not listed this. Yet I begin to feel now that too much has been made of what is not there. Before the book appeared, I looked again at early manuscript and printed editions of the *Description of the World* and began to feel that I should have laid far more stress on these and that such textual material need not present a barrier to popular enjoyment. Indeed, in discussing omissions, in using modern versions of the text, cobbled together from a great variety of versions, I was laying something of a false trail.

Take the description of Fuzhou. This, mainly because of its interesting account of the Manicheans (wrongly described by "Marco Polo" as Christians), is a key passage. Yet this key passage occurs first in the mid–fifteenth century Toledo manuscript, copied more than a hundred years after Marco Polo's death. In the printed edition of Nuremburg (1477), in Frampton's English version (printed in 1579), in the Bodleian manuscript (Mss. Bodley 264) of circa 1400, in a Venetian dialect manuscript of 1457 (Sloan 251), and numerous other early versions, there is a single paragraph on Fuzhou, describing the river and the maritime trade and nothing else.

Similarly, the description of Hangzhou in all these early versions is only two pages long and does not include the material from the letter written by the "Queen of Manzi" to Bayan which expands later versions of the description of Hangzhou into many pages.

The original version of the text has disappeared. The early versions are short: the Venetian manuscript has 39 folios, the Bodleian (with its wonderful illustrations), 58. The late appearance of some of the "best" material must suggest that it was added by later copyists or publishers (like Ramusio) who had access to more material on China which they felt could be usefully incorporated. It would have been helpful if the material had been acknowledged (and dated), but as it stands, it has nothing to do with Marco Polo and his original text. Marco Polo did not see or describe Manicheans in Fuzhou nor did he personally include the Queen of Manzi's letter in any early version of his text. In the absence of the original manuscript, it is difficult to know what he did or did not see, but careful comparisons of the earliest versions reveal a far slimmer account than is popularly assumed.

Crediting Polo himself with all these later additions has helped to create the myth of the great observer which is simply not tenable on the basis of early versions of *The Description of the World.*

Notes

Introduction

1 Colonel Sir Henry Yule, *The Travels of Marco Polo: the complete Yule-Cordier edition* (1903, 1920; New York, 1993), vol. 1, pp. 4–6.
2 Herbert Franke, 'Sino-Western relations under the Mongol Empire', *Journal of the Royal Asiatic Society Hong Kong Branch*, 6 (Hong Kong, 1966), pp. 49–72, reprinted in a collected volume of Franke's work *China Under Mongol Rule* (Aldershot, 1994). For a bibliography, see H. Watanabe, *Marco Polo Bibliography 1477–1983* (Tokyo, 1986).

1 The Bare Details

1 This quotation and quotations of Marco Polo throughout are taken from Ronald Latham's translation of *Discovery of the World*: Ronald Latham, *Marco Polo: The Travels* (Harmondsworth, 1958).

2 Why go at all?

1 F. Fernandez-Arnesto, *Columbus* (Oxford, 1991), p. 39.
2 Ronald Latham, *Marco Polo: The Travels* (Harmondsworth, 1958), p. 217.
3 Donald Lach, *Asia in the Making of Europe* (Chicago, 1965), vol. 1, p. 20.
4 Ibid., vol. 1, p. 15.
5 Ibid., vol. 1, p. 21.
6 *The Silk Book* (London, 1951), pp. 14, 90
7 Roberto Sabatinio Lopez, 'China Silk in Europe in the

Yuan Period', *Journal of the American Oriental Society,* 72, (New Haven, 1952), p. 75.

8 A. C. Moule and Paul Pelliot, *Marco Polo: The Travels* (London, 1938), vol. 1, p. 524 and Phillips, *Medieval Expansion,* p. 93.

9 J. Keay, *The Honourable Company* (London, 1993), pp. 18, 52–3, 61.

10 Aubrey Singer, *The Lion and the Dragon* (London, 1992), p. 181.

11 Jacques Heers, *Marco Polo* (Paris, 1982), pp. 30–1.

12 L. Petech, 'Les marchands italiens dans l'empire Mongole', *Journal Asiatique* (Paris, 1962), p. 551.

13 Petech, 'Les marchands', p. 552 and John Critchley, *Marco Polo's Book* (Aldershot, 1992), pp. 48–9.

14 Petech, 'Les marchands', p. 556.

15 F. Rouleau, 'The Yangchow Latin tombstone as a landmark of medieval Christianity in China', *Harvard Journal of Asiatic Studies,* 17, Cambridge, Mass., 1954, p. 363.

16 Igor de Rachewiltz, *Papal Envoys to the Great Khans* (London, 1971), p. 182.

17 Singer, *The Lion,* p. 4.

18 Colonel Sir Henry Yule, *Cathay and the Way Thither* (London, 1916), pp. 291–2.

19 Petech, 'Les marchands', p. 557.

20 R. Gallo, 'Marco Polo, la sua famiglia ed il suo libro', *Nel VII centario della nascità di Marco Polo* (Venice, 1955), pp. 447–52.

21 Moule and Pelliot, *Marco Polo,* vol. 1, p. 316.

3 Missionaries nose to tail

1 J. P. Desroches, *Visiteurs de l'Empire Celeste* (Paris, 1994), pp. 72–7. Alastair Lamb suggested that one of the most accessible guides to the religious correspondence and activity of the period is Christopher Henry Dawson's *The Mongol Mission: Narratives and letters of the Franciscan missionaries to Mongolia and China in the 13th and 14th centuries* (London and New York, 1955).

2 Samuel Couling, *Encyclopaedia Sinica (1917)* (Hong Kong, 1983), p. 327.

3 C. R. Beazley (ed.), *The Text and Versions of John de Plano Carpine and William de Rubruquis* (London, 1903), p. 107.

4 Igor de Rachewiltz, *Papal Envoys to the Great Khans* (London, 1971), p. 90.

5 Ibid., p. 92.

6 David Morgan, *The Mongols* (Oxford, 1986), pp. 137–9 and J. R. S. Phillips, *The Medieval Expansion of Europe* (Oxford, 1988), p. 69.

7 *Grand Larousse Encyclopédique* (Paris, 1964), vol. 10, pp. 833–4.

8 Peter Jackson, *The Mission of William of Rubruck* (London, 1990), p. 42.

9 Ibid., p. 51.

10 Ibid., p. 221.

11 A. C. Moule and Paul Pelliot, *Marco Polo: The Travels* (London, 1938), vol. 1, p. 524 and Phillips, *Medieval Expansion*, p. 93.

12 Ronald Latham, *Marco Polo: The Travels* (Harmondsworth, 1958), p. 92.

13 Colonel Sir Henry Yule, *Cathay and the Way Thither* (London, 1916), pp. 197–209. Jack Dabbs identifies him as Johannes Vitodoranus, see Dabbs, *History of the Discovery and Exploration of Chinese Turkestan* (Hague, 1963), p. 19.

14 Latham, *Marco Polo*, p. 234 and Yule, *Cathay*, pp. 106–7.

15 Yule, *Cathay*, pp. 144–6. The fern is, apparently, native to China, see Mark Jones (ed.), *Fake? The Art of Deception* (London, 1990), p. 85.

4 Prester John and the Magi

1 R. W. Southern, *The Making of the Middle Ages* (London, 1967), p. 67.

2 John Goodall, *Heaven and Earth: 120 album leaves from a Ming encyclopaedia* (London, 1979).

3 Leonardo Olschki, *Marco Polo's Asia* (Berkeley, 1960), p. 382.

4 Donald Lach, *Asia in the Making of Europe* (Chicago, 1965), vol. 1, pp. 25–6.
5 Olschki, *Marco Polo's Asia*, p. 383.
6 Igor de Rachewiltz, *Papal Envoys to the Great Khans* (London, 1971), p. 31.
7 Ibid., p. 35.
8 Ronald Latham, *Marco Polo: The Travels* (Harmondsworth, 1958), pp. 93–6.
9 Rachewiltz, *Papal Envoys*, p. 42.
10 Paul Pelliot, *Notes on Marco Polo* (Paris, 1959–63), vol. II, p. 850.
11 Latham, *Marco Polo*, p. 106.
12 Ibid., p. 22.
13 Olschki, *Marco Polo's Asia*, p. 192.
14 Ibid., p. 228.
15 Latham, *Marco Polo*, pp. 274–6.
16 Olschki, *Marco Polo's Asia*, pp. 228–9.
17 Rachewiltz, *Papal Envoys*, pp. 117–18.
18 Latham, *Marco Polo*, pp. 58–9.
19 A. C. Moule and Paul Pelliot, *Marco Polo: The Travels* (London, 1938), vol. I, p. 350.
20 S. N. C. Lieu, *Manichaeism in the Later Roman Empire and Medieval China* (Tubingen, 1992), pp. 297–8.
21 Olschki, *Marco Polo's Asia*, p. 204.
22 Sir Stephen Runiciman, *The Medieval Manichee* (Cambridge, 1947).
23 John Critchley, *Marco Polo's Book* (Aldershot, 1992), pp. 148–57.

5 Not an itinerary

1 See, for example, Jin Buhong, *In the Footsteps of Marco Polo* (Peking, 1989).
2 Ronald Latham, *Marco Polo: The Travels* (Harmondsworth, 1958), p. 51.
3 Ibid., p. 62.
4 Ibid., p. 87.
5 Ibid., p. 330.
6 Ibid., p. 165.

7 Ibid., p. 259.

8 Colonel Sir Henry Yule, *The Travels of Marco Polo: the complete Yule-Cordier edition* (1903, 1920; New York, 1993), vol. 2, p. 107.

9 Ibid., vol. 2, p. 117.

10 Ibid., vol. 2, p. 130.

11 Latham, *Marco Polo*, p. 312.

12 Francis Woodman Cleaves, 'A Chinese source bearing upon Marco Polo's departure from China and a Persian source on his arrival in Persia', *Harvard Journal of Asiatic Studies*, 36 (Cambridge, Mass., 1976), pp. 181–203.

13 Yang Zhijiu, 'Make Poluo li hua de yi duan hanwen jicai' in Xu Shixiong, *Make Poluo jieshao yu yanjiu* (Peking, 1983), pp. 169–78.

14 Cleaves, 'A Chinese source', p. 192.

15 The texts are generally broken up into short sections but for convenience, I am following the chapter headings used by Latham in his edition *Marco Polo: The Travels*.

16 Latham, *Marco Polo*, p. 46.

17 Ibid., p. 58.

18 Ibid., p. 60.

19 Ibid., p. 65.

20 Ibid., pp. 77–8.

21 According to Yule, 'an expression on which no light has been thrown since Ramusio's time,' but which he nevertheless defines as 'a sort of steel of surpassing value and excellence'. Colonel Sir Henry Yule, *The Travels of Marco Polo: the complete Yule-Cordier edition* (1903, 1920; New York, 1993), vol. 1, p. 93.

22 Latham, *Marco Polo*, p. 89.

23 Ibid., pp. 89–90.

24 Ibid., p. 92.

25 Ibid., p. 163.

26 Ibid., p. 201.

27 Ibid., p. 199.

28 Ibid., p. 206.

29 Ibid., pp. 207–8.

30 Ibid., p. 213.

31 Jacques Gernet, *Daily Life in China on the Eve of the Mongol Conquest* (Stanford, 1970), pp. 19, 30, 38.
32 Latham, *Marco Polo*, p. 240.
33 Ibid., p. 254.
34 Ibid., p. 266.
35 Ibid., p. 264.
36 A. C. Moule and Paul Pelliot, *Marco Polo: The Travels* (London, 1938), vol. II, pp. xv–xvi.
37 Ibid., p. vi.
38 Ibid., p. viii.
39 Italo Calvino, *Invisible Cities* (London, 1974), p. 5.

6 The ghost writer and the first fan

1 Ronald Latham, *Marco Polo: The Travels* (Harmondsworth, 1958), pp. 33–4. Professor Barbara Wehr, daughter of a famous arabist and herself a Romance specialist, has recently taken up the subject of language and transmission in Polo's text. Apropos Rustichello and ghost writing, I am informed that one German academic thinks that Rustichello may have invented Marco Polo.
2 Colonel Sir Henry Yule, *The Travels of Marco Polo: the complete Yule-Cordier edition* (1903, 1920; New York, 1993), vol. 1, p. 58 and John Critchley, *Marco Polo's Book* (Aldershot, 1992), pp. 2–8.
3 Luigi Foscolo Benedetto, *Il Milione* (Florence, 1928), p. xviii.
4 Michael Prestwich, *Edward I* (London, 1988), p. 6.
5 Ibid., p. 118.
6 Ibid., p. 118.
7 Ibid., p. 120.
8 Leonardo Olschki (ed.), *Il Milione* (Firenze, 1928).
9 Yule, *The Travels*, vol. 1, pp. 5–6. See also Sir Edward Denison Ross, 'Marco Polo and his Book' (London, 1935).
10 Latham, *Marco Polo*, p. 33.
11 Jacques Heers, *Marco Polo* (Paris, 1982), pp. 277–8.
12 Ramusio, quoted in Yule, *The Travels*, vol. 1, p. 4.

13 Thirteenth-century author of the *Imago Mundi*, a collection of travellers' tales, quoted in Luigi Foscolo Benedetto, *Il Milione* (Florence, 1928), p. cxciv.

14 Latham, *Marco Polo*, p. 33.

15 A. C. Moule and Paul Pelliot, *Marco Polo: The Travels* (London, 1938), vol. 1, pp. 509–520; and Shinobu Iwamura, *Manuscripts and Printed Editions of Marco Polo's Travels* (Tokyo, 1949).

16 Benedetto, *Il Milione*, p. xxxix.

17 Latham, *Marco Polo*, pp. 24–5.

18 Benedetto, *Il Milione*, p. lxxv. His list is summarised with the inclusion of the Toledo manuscript in Moule and Pelliot, *Marco Polo*, vol. 2, p. 509.

19 Ibid., p. cix. Ramusio said the version was produced in 1320, though according to Yule citing Pipino it was possibly slightly earlier, some time after 1315, see Yule, *The Travels*, vol. 1, p. 25.

20 C. W. R. D. Moseley (ed.), *The Travels of Sir John Mandeville* (Harmondsworth, 1983), p. 9.

21 Jack Beeching (ed.), *Richard Hakluyt: Voyages and Discoveries* (Harmondsworth, 1983), p. 19.

22 Latham, *Marco Polo*, p. 16.

23 Ibid., p. 58.

24 Ibid., p. 96.

25 Moule and Pelliot, *Marco Polo*, vol. 1, pp. 205, 206.

26 Ibid., vol. 1, p. 49.

27 Latham, *Marco Polo*, pp. 25–6.

28 Critchley, *Marco Polo's Book*, p. 12 *et seq.*

29 J. P. Desroches, *Visiteurs de l'Empire Celeste* (Paris, 1994), plate 18.

30 R. Wittkower, 'Marco Polo and the pictorial tradition of the Marvels of the East' in R. Wittkower, *Allegory and the Migration of Symbols* (London, 1977).

7 The language of the text

1 Hugh Murray, *The Travels of Marco Polo* (Edinburgh, 1847), p. 27.

2 Jacques Heers, *Marco Polo* (Paris, 1982), p. 293.

3 Ibid., p. 293.

4 M. G. Capuzzo, 'La Lingua del Divisament dou Monde di Marco Polo, 1, Morfologia Verbale', *Biblioteca degli Studii Mediolatini e Volgari* (new ser.), v (Pisa, 1980), p. 33 and John Critchley, *Marco Polo's Book* (Aldershot, 1992), pp. 12–19. See also Robert Hughes, *Barcelona* (London, 1992), pp. 58–9.

5 Peter Hopkirk, *Foreign Devils on the Silk Road* (London, 1980). It is to Peter Hopkirk that I owe much encouragement, for being surprised at my first mention of Polo's possible non-visit, and for continuing to be interested for almost twenty years.

6 Quotations and content of this chapter are very much based on Paul Pelliot, *Notes on Marco Polo* (Paris, 1959–63).

7 Leonardo Olschki, *Marco Polo's Asia* (Berkeley, 1960), p. 81.

8 Ibid., pp. 86–7.

9 A. C. Moule and Paul Pelliot, *Marco Polo: The Travels* (London, 1938), vol. 3, p. 349.

10 Igor de Rachewiltz, *Papal Envoys to the Great Khans* (London, 1971), p. 102.

11 Ibid., p. 103.

12 J. R. S. Phillips, *The Medieval Expansion of Europe* (Oxford, 1988), p. 77.

13 Pelliot, *Notes,* vol. 1, pp. 805–12.

14 I. and J.-L. Vissière (eds.), *Lettres edifiantes et curieuses de Chine par des missionaires jésuites 1702–1776* (Paris, 1979), p. 183.

15 Pelliot, *Notes,* vol. 1, p. 808.

16 Ronald Latham, *Marco Polo: The Travels* (Harmondsworth, 1958), pp. 317–8.

17 Pelliot, *Notes,* vol. 1, p. 831.

18 Latham, *Marco Polo,* p. 319.

19 *Cihai* dictionary: the appearance of father and son in this suggests a reasonably prominent position in Chinese popular history, perhaps because of the occasional anti-Mongol stance.

20 Pelliot, *Notes,* vol. 1, p. 781.
21 Latham, *Marco Polo,* p. 132.
22 Pelliot, *Notes,* vol. 1, p. 781.
23 Latham, *Marco Polo,* p. 244.
24 Moule and Pelliot, *Marco Polo,* vol. 1, p. 93.

8 Omissions and Inclusions

1 Herbert Franke, 'Sino-Western relations under the Mongol Empire', *Journal of the Royal Asiatic Society Hong Kong Branch,* 6, Hong Kong, 1966, pp. 49–72.
2 Böttger of the Meissen factory finally succeeded in the mid eighteenth century: see Margaret Medley, *The Chinese Potter* (Oxford, 1980), p. 261.
3 A. C. Moule and Paul Pelliot, *Marco Polo: The Travels* (London, 1938), vol. 2, p. 352.
4 Shelagh Vainker, *Chinese Pottery and Porcelain* (London, 1991), p. 143.
5 Rose Kerr and Penelope Hughes-Stanton. *Kiln Sites of Ancient China* (London, 1980), pp. 22–38.
6 Ibid., pp. 26–9.
7 See John Ayers, 'Blanc de Chine', *Transactions of the Oriental Ceramic Society,* 51 (London, 1986–87), pp. 16–17.
8 Moule and Pelliot, *Marco Polo,* vol. 1, p. 238.
9 Colonel Sir Henry Yule, *Cathay and the Way Thither* (London, 1916), vol. 4, p. 113.
10 Tsien Tsuen-hsuin, 'Paper and Printing', in J. Needham (ed.), *Science and Civilisation in China,* vol. 5, part 1 (Cambridge, 1985), p. 299.
11 Moule and Pelliot, *Marco Polo,* vol. 1, p. 238.
12 Peter Jackson, *The Mission of William of Rubruck* (London, 1990), p. 203.
13 Ibid., p. 203.
14 Leonardo Olschki, *Marco Polo's Asia* (Berkeley, 1960), p. 139.
15 M. Rossabi, *Khubilai Khan* (Berkeley, 1988), p. 154.
16 D. C. Twitchett, *Printing and Publishing in Medieval China* (London, 1983), p. 12.

17 Rossabi, *Khubilai Khan,* p. 15.
18 Herbert Franke, 'Could the Mongol Emperors read and write Chinese?', *Asia Major,* new series, 3, 1 (London, 1932), p. 30.
19 Moule and Pelliot, *Marco Polo,* vol. 1, p. 337.
20 Twitchett, *Printing and Publishing,* pp. 45–52.
21 Jacques Gernet, *Daily Life in China on the Eve of the Mongol Conquest* (Stanford, 1970), p. 49.
22 Latham, *Marco Polo,* p. 217.
23 See P. B. Ebrey, *The Inner Quarters: marriage and the lives of Chinese women in the Sung period* (Berkeley, 1993).
24 Ebrey, *The Inner Quarters,* pp. 26–7.
25 Yule, *Cathay,* vol. 1, p. 153.
26 Ibid., vol. 1, p. 153.
27 C. W. R. D. Moseley (ed.), *The Travels of Sir John Mandeville* (Harmondsworth, 1983), p. 187.
28 Sir John Barrow, *Travels in China* (London, 1804), pp. 506–7.
29 Yule, *Cathay,* vol. 1, p. 112.
30 Barrow, *Travels,* pp. 75–7.
31 Sir George Staunton, *An authentic account of the embassy from the King of Great Britain to the Emperor of China* (Dublin, 1798).

9 Ice-cream and spaghetti

1 Aeneas Anderson, *A Narrative of the British Embassy to China* (London, 1795), p. 81.
2 Verbal communication, Dr Albertine Gaur.
3 For *The Food of Italy.*
4 Claudia Roden, *The Food of Italy* (London, 1989), pp. 176–9.
5 Ibid., p. 26.
6 Chang Kwang-chih, *Food in Chinese Culture* (New Haven, 1977), p. 7.
7 W. Watson (ed.), *The Genius of China* (London, 1973), p. 133.
8 For Mongol dietary terms see Yan-shuan Lao, 'Notes on non-Chinese terms in the Yuan imperial dietary

compendium *Yinshan zhengyao'* in *Bulletin of the Institute of History and Philology, Academia Sinica,* vol. xxxix, pp. 399–416, Taipei, 1969; and Herbert Franke, 'Additional notes on non-Chinese terms in the Yuan imperial dietary compendium *Yinshan zhengyao'* in *Zentralasiatische Studien,* 4 (Wiesbaden, 1970), pp. 7–16. Caroline Liddell and Robin Weir, *Ices* (London, 1993), p. 10.

9 Ibid., pp. 10–11.
10 Ibid., p. 11.

10 Walls within walls

1 L. Sickman and A. Soper. *The Art and Architecture of China* (Harmondsworth, 1971), pp. 400, 410–20.
2 Ronald Latham, *Marco Polo: The Travels* (Harmondsworth, 1958), p. 128. Franke notes that white, though an inauspicious colour for the Chinese, was an auspicious colour for the Mongols and used notably in the Baita si (White stupa temple) consecrated in Peking in 1279. See Franke's article thereupon in *Asia Minor* (forthcoming).
3 Ibid., p. 128.
4 J. Needham (ed.), *Science and Civilisation in China,* vol. 2, (Cambridge, 1985), p. 360.
5 Latham, *Marco Polo,* p. 126.
6 Ibid., p. 126.
7 Ibid., p. 125.
8 A. C. Moule and Paul Pelliot, *Marco Polo: The Travels* (London, 1938), vol. 2, pp. 255–6.
9 Ibid., p. 256.
10 Colonel Sir Henry Yule, *The Travels of Marco Polo: the complete Yule-Cordier edition* (1903, 1920; New York, 1993), vol. 2, p. 6.
11 Latham, *Marco Polo,* p. 129.
12 Ibid., p. 212.
13 Yule, *The Travels,* vol. 2, p. 183.
14 However, he only did so in the ever-helpful Toledo version and one Venetian manuscript: see Moule and Pelliot, *Marco Polo,* vol. 1, p. 327.

15 Yule, *The Travels*, vol. 2, p. 194.
16 Jacques Gernet, *Daily Life in China on the Eve of the Mongol Conquest* (Stanford, 1970), p. 124.
17 Ibid., p. 31.
18 Yule, *The Travels*, vol. 2, p. 210.
19 Gernet, *Daily Life*, p. 31.
20 Ibid., p. 34.
21 A. B. Freeman-Mitford, *The Attaché at Peking* (London, 1900), p. 61.
22 Gernet, *Daily Life*, pp. 31–2.
23 Ibid., pp. 34–5.
24 Demao Kong, *The Mansion of Confucius* (London, 1989), p. 113.
25 By Jacques Gernet in *Daily Life*.
26 Latham, *Marco Polo*, p. 206.

11 He missed the biggest wall

1 Arthur N. Waldron, 'The problem of the Great Wall', *Harvard Journal of Asiatic Studies*, 43/2 (Cambridge, Mass., 1983), p. 645 and Fan Tsen-chung, 'Dr Johnson and Chinese Culture', in *Nine Dragon Screen* (London, 1945), pp. 15–18, where he suggests that Johnson's inspiration may have been Du Halde.
2 James Boswell, *The Life of Johnson* (London, 1933), vol. 2, p. 193.
3 Sir George Staunton, *An authentic account of the embassy from the King of Great Britain to the Emperor of China* (Dublin, 1798), vol. 2, p. 73.
4 Waldron, 'The problem of the Great Wall', p. 656.
5 Staunton, *An authentic account*, vol. 2, p. 78.
6 Waldron, 'The problem of the Great Wall', pp. 643–63.

12 Not unique and certainly not a siege engineer

1 Herbert Franke, 'Sino-Western relations under the Mongol Empire', *Journal of the Royal Asiatic Society Hong Kong Branch*, 6, Hong Kong, 1966, pp. 54–5.

2 Leonardo Olschki, *Guillaume Boucher: a French artist at the court of the Khans* (Baltimore, 1946), from where I have taken the Rubruck quotations. Leonardo Olschki's scholarship was wide-ranging, but is not well enough known; *Guillaume Boucher* merits reprinting – its appearance after the War means that too few libraries hold the original. I am grateful to his nephew Mr Rosenthal for showing me Arthur R. Evans' article, 'Leonardo Olschki, 1885–1961', in *Romance Philosophy*, xxxi/i, Stanford, 1977.

3 David Morgan, *The Mongols* (Oxford, 1986), pp. 137–9 and J. R. S. Phillips, *The Medieval Expansion of Europe* (Oxford, 1988), p. 61.

4 Ibid., p. 125.

5 Leonardo Olschki, *Marco Polo's Asia* (Berkeley, 1960), p. 67.

6 Morgan, *The Mongols,* p. 116.

7 Olschki, *Guillaume Boucher,* for further quotations from Rubruck and for the description of the wine-dispensing machine.

8 Chen Yuan, *Western and Central Asians in China Under the Mongols* (Los Angeles, 1966), p. 221.

9 Ibid., p. 219.

10 C. P. Fitzgerald, *Barbarian Beds: the origin of the chair in China* (London, 1965).

11 Chen, *Western and Central Asians,* p. 221.

12 Ibid., p. 221.

13 Morgan, *The Mongols,* p. 84.

14 E. O. Reischauer and J. K. Fairbank, *East Asia: the Great Tradition* (Boston, 1960), p. 266.

15 M. Rossabi, *Khubilai Khan* (Berkeley, 1988), p. 125.

16 Ibid., p. 86.

17 Ronald Latham, *Marco Polo: The Travels* (Harmondsworth, 1958), pp. 207–8.

18 A. C. Moule and Paul Pelliot, *Marco Polo: The Travels* (London, 1938), vol. 1, p. 27.

19 J. A. G. Boyle, *The Successors of Genghis Kahn* (New York, 1971), pp. 290–1.

20 C. W. R. D. Moseley (ed.), *The Travels of Sir John Mandeville* (Harmondsworth, 1983), p. 144.

21 Morgan, *The Mongols*, p. 160.

22 Michael Prestwich, *Edward I* (London, 1988), p. 330. See also Sir E. A. Wallis Budge, *The Monks of Kublai Khan . . . on the history of the life and travels of Rabban Sauma* (London, 1928).

13 Who were the Polos?

1 A Geographical compilation made by a rough contemporary of Marco Polo's.

2 British Library, Additional MS 12475.

3 Colonel Sir Henry Yule, *The Travels of Marco Polo: the complete Yule-Cordier edition* (1903, 1920; New York, 1993), vol. 1, p. 78.

4 A. C. Moule and Paul Pelliot, *Marco Polo: The Travels* (London, 1938), vol. 2, pp. 17–19.

5 Yule, *The Travels*, vol. 2, pp. 17–19.

6 Moule and Pelliot, *Marco Polo*, vol. 2, pp. 15–19.

7 Leonardo Olschki, *Marco Polo's Asia* (Berkeley, 1960), p. 100.

8 J. R. S. Phillips, *The Medieval Expansion of Europe* (Oxford, 1988), p. 20.

9 Sir Mark Aurel Stein, *Ruins of Desert Cathay* (London, 1912; New York, 1987), p. 518. On the problems of horse-breeding, see Austin Coates, *China Races* (Hong Kong, 1994), p. 3; for sheep, see Jack Dabbs, *History of the Discovery and Exploration of Chinese Turkestan*, Central Asiatic Studies VIII (Hague, 1963), p. 92.

10 Ibid., p. 518.

11 David Morgan, *The Mongols* (Oxford, 1986), p. 23.

12 Moule and Pelliot, *Marco Polo*, vol. 1, p. 82.

13 Yule, *The Travels*, vol. 1, pp. 351–6.

14 Polo, Marco. *Il libro di Marco Polo detto Milione* (Turin, 1954), pp. 5, 13.

15 Aldo Ricci (trans.), *The Travels of Marco Polo* (London, 1931), p. 17.

16 Yule, *The Travels,* vol. 1, p. 353.

17 William Dalrymple, *In Xanadu: a quest* (London, 1990), pp. 298–9.

14 Was it China?

1 Ronald Latham, *Marco Polo: The Travels* (Harmondsworth, 1958), p. 122.

2 Ibid., pp. 122-3. Professor Franke notes that here, again, Polo is certainly right but mixes things up a bit, for the Mongol Khans always married (as first wives) girls from the Oonggirad (Polo's Kungarat) tribe; a form of marriage alliance that dated back to the twelfth century and lasted until 1368. Concubines were not of restricted provenance.

3 Ibid., p. 135.

4 Ibid., p. 136.

5 Ibid., p. 136–45.

6 M. Rossabi, *Khubilai Khan* (Berkeley, 1988), p. 215.

7 Latham, *Marco Polo,* pp. 176–7, 194, 228.

8 Ibid., pp. 178, 205.

9 Ibid., pp. 173–4.

10 Jacques Gernet, *Daily Life in China on the Eve of the Mongol Conquest* (Stanford, 1970), pp. 80–1.

11 Latham, *Marco Polo,* p. 42.

12 Luigi Foscolo Benedetto, *Il Milione* (Florence, 1928), p. cxciii.

13 Leonardo Olschki, *Marco Polo's Asia* (Berkeley, 1960), p. 103.

14 A. C. Moule and Paul Pelliot, *Marco Polo: The Travels* (London, 1938), vol. 2, pp. 73–4.

15 Moule and Pelliot, *Marco Polo,* vol. 2, p. 35.

16 Ibid., vol. 2, pp. 29, 35.

17 Herbert Franke, 'Sino-Western relations under the Mongol Empire', *Journal of the Royal Asiatic Society Hong Kong Branch,* 6, Hong Kong, 1966, pp. 49–72.

18 Moule and Pelliot, *Marco Polo,* vol. 2, p. 37.

19 Leonardo Olschki, *Marco Polo's Asia* (Berkeley, 1960), pp. 104–5.

20 Colonel Sir Henry Yule, *The Travels of Marco Polo: the complete Yule-Cordier edition* (1903, 1920; New York, 1993), vol. 1, p. 67.

21 Moule and Pelliot, *Marco Polo*, vol. 1, p. 30.

22 Ibid., vol. 1, p. 539.

23 Ibid., vol. 1, p. 542.

24 R. Vaughan, *The illustrated chronicles of Matthew Paris*, Stroud, 1993, p. ix.

25 David Morgan, *The Mongols* (Oxford, 1986), p. 57.

26 Ibid., pp. 142, 160–3, 124.

27 Latham, *Marco Polo*, p. 101.

28 Jacques Heers, *Marco Polo* (Paris, 1982), pp. 34–5.

29 Moule and Pelliot, *Marco Polo*, vol. 1, p. 555.

30 Olschki, *Marco Polo's Asia*, p. 157.

31 John Gittings, *A Chinese View of China* (London, 1973), pp. 43–50.

32 Peter Jackson, *The Mission of William of Rubruck* (London, 1990), p. 217.

33 I am indebted to Sir Matthew Farrar for an interest in the number of these gold tables which sent me back to the texts, where I found the confusion of numbers ever deepening.

15 A significant absence

1 Herbert Franke, 'Sino-Western relations under the Mongol Empire', *Journal of the Royal Asiatic Society Hong Kong Branch*, 6, Hong Kong, 1966, p. 5.

2 In an essay by Professor Yang Zhijiu, included in Yu Shixiong's *Make Poluo jieshao yu yanjiu (Introduction and research into Marco Polo)* (Peking, 1983), pp. 280–1.

3 *Ershisishi jizhuan renming suoyin* (Peking, 1980).

4 *Yuan shi, juan* 205.

5 Paul Pelliot, review of Charignon's re-edition of Pauthier's *Le Livre de Marco Polo*, in *T'oung Pao*, 25 (Leiden, 1927), p. 157 and Leonardo Olschki, 'Une question d'onomatologie chinoise', *Oriens,* 3 (Leiden, 1950), p. 158.

6 I should not really mention Matthews in the same paragraph as Paul Pelliot, for students of Chinese are

taught to eschew this missionary dictionary produced in
1931. To be fair to Matthews, his famous inaccuracies are
mostly to do with a prim unwillingness to mention sex or
concubinage, so concubines always appear as wives, sisters
or great-nieces, which can considerably confuse family
relations.

7 Olschki, 'Une question d'onomatologie chinoise', p. 189.
8 Ibid., p. 189.
9 Herbert Franke, 'European in der Ostasiatischen
Geschichtschreibung des 13 und 14 Jahrhunderts',
Saeculum, 11 (Freiburg in the Breisgau, 1951), pp. 65–75.
10 J. A. G. Boyle, 'Rashid al-Din and the Franks', in Boyle,
The Mongol World Empire (London, 1977).
11 Francis Woodman Cleaves, 'A Chinese source bearing
upon Marco Polo's departure from China and a Persian
source on his arrival in Persia', *Harvard Journal of Asiatic
Studies*, 36 (Cambridge, Mass., 1976), pp. 181–203.
12 Yang Zhijiu 'Make Poluo yu Zhongguo' in Xu Shixiong,
Make Poluo jieshao yu yanjiu (Peking, 1983), pp. 52–60.
13 John Haeger, 'Marco Polo in China? Problems with
internal evidence', *Bulletin of Sung-Yuan Studies*, 14 (New
York, 1979), pp. 22–30.
14 Craig Clunas, 'Did Marco Polo get to China?', *The Times*,
14 April 1982.

Conclusion

1 Clarence Dalrymple Bruce, *In the Footsteps of Marco Polo*
(London, 1907), p. 171.
2 Translation by Juan Gil, Madrid, Testimonio, 1986.
3 C. W. R. D. Moseley (ed.), *The Travels of Sir John Mandeville*
(Harmondsworth, 1983), pp. 9–10.
4 Ibid., p. 9.
5 Ibid., pp. 9, 33.
6 Ibid., p. 19.
7 Colonel Sir Henry Yule, *Cathay and the Way Thither*
(London, 1916), p. 125.

8 Herbert Franke, 'Sino-Western relations under the Mongol Empire', *Journal of the Royal Asiatic Society Hong Kong Branch*, 6, Hong Kong, 1966, p. 54.

9 Translated into French by Abbé Renaud in his *Anciennes Relations de l'Inde at de la Chine de deux voyageurs Mahoumetans qui y allèrent dans le IXe siècle, 1718*, see Yule, p. 125.

10 J. A. G. Boyle, 'Rashid al-Din and the Franks', in Boyle, *The Mongol World Empire* (London, 1977).

11 Herbert Franke, 'Some Sinological remarks on Rashid al-Din's History of China', *Oriens*, 4/1 (Leiden, 1951), p. 21.

12 Ibid., p. 23. For details of Rashid al-Din's historical writing, see also Bernard Lewis, *The Muslim Discovery of Europe* (London, 1994), especially pp. 150–7.

13 Ibid., p. 23.

14 Yule, *Cathay*, p. 112.

15 Ibid., pp. 110–13.

16 Ibid., p. 110.

17 Yule, *Cathay*, pp. 129–137.

18 Ronald Latham, *Marco Polo: The Travels* (Harmondsworth, 1958), p. 234.

19 Ursula Sims-Williams, verbal communication.

20 John Critchley, *Marco Polo's Book* (Aldershot, 1992), p. 10.

21 Jarl Charpentier (ed.), *The Livro de Seita dos Indios Orientais of Father Jacobo Fenicio* (Uppsala, 1933), p. xi. Thanks also to Maurice Smith for raising Herodotus and similar useful references when I taught him Chinese literature. He rescued me from a virtual lynching by fellow students who could not tolerate the political force of Cultural Revolution literature by mentioning Shaw in the same gentle manner.

Bibliography

Anderson, Aeneas. *A Narrative of the British Embassy to China,* London, 1795.

Ayers, John. 'Blanc de Chine', *Transactions of the Oriental Ceramic Society,* 51, London, 1986–7.

Barrow, Sir John. *Travels in China,* London, 1804.

Beazley, C. R. (ed.). *The Text and Versions of John de Plano Carpine and William de Rubruquis,* London, 1903.

Beeching, Jack (ed.). *Richard Hakluyt: Voyages and Discoveries,* Harmondsworth, 1983.

Benedetto, Luigi Foscolo. *Il Milione,* Florence, 1928.

Boswell, James. *The Life of Johnson,* London, 1933.

Boyle, J. A. G. 'Rashid al-Din and the Franks', in J. A. G. Boyle, *The Mongol World Empire,* London, 1977.

The Successors of Genghis Kahn, New York, 1971.

British Library, Additional MS 12475.

Bruce, Clarence Dalrymple. *In the Footsteps of Marco Polo,* London, 1907.

Budge, Sir E. A. Wallis. *The Monks of Kublai Khan . . . on the history of the life and travels of Rabban Sauma,* London, 1928.

Calvino, Italo. *Invisible Cities,* London, 1974.

Capuzzo, M. G. 'La Lingua del Divisament deu Monde di Marco Polo, 1, Morfologia Verbale', *Biblioteca degli Studii Mediolatini e Volgari* (new series), v, Pisa, 1980.

Chang Kwang-chih. *Food in Chinese Culture,* New Haven, 1977.

Charpentier, Jarl (ed.). *The Livro de Seita dos Indios Orientais of Father Jacobo Fenicio,* Uppsala, 1933.

Chen Yuan. *Western and Central Asians in China Under the Mongols,* Los Angeles, 1966.

Cleaves, Frances Woodman. 'A Chinese source bearing upon Marco Polo's departure from China and a Persian source on his arrival in Persia', *Harvard Journal of Asiatic Studies,* 36, Cambridge, Mass., 1976.

Coates, Austin. *China Races,* Hong Kong, 1994.

Couling, Samuel. *Encyclopaedia Sinica* (Shanghai, 1917), Hong Kong, 1983.

Critchley, John. *Marco Polo's Book,* Aldershot, 1992.

Dabbs, Jack A. *History of the Discovery and Exploration of Chinese Turkestan,* Central Asiatic Studies VIII, Hague, 1963.

Dalrymple, William. *In Xanadu: a quest,* London, 1990.

Dawson, Christopher Henry. *The Mongol Mission: Narratives and letters of the Franciscan missionaries to Mongolia and China in the 13th and 14th centuries,* London and New York, 1955.

Desroches, J. P. *Visiteurs de l'Empire Celeste,* Paris, 1994.

Ebrey, P. B. *The Inner Quarters: marriage and the lives of Chinese women in the Sung period,* Berkeley, 1993.

Evans, Arthur R. 'Leonardo Olschki 1885–1961', *Romance Philosophy,* xxxi/i, Stanford, 1977.

Fan, Tseng-chung. 'Dr Johnson and Chinese culture' in *Nine Dragon Screen,* London, 1965.

Fernandez-Armesto, F. *Columbus,* Oxford, 1991.

Fitzgerald, C. P. *Barbarian Beds: the origin of the chair in China,* London, 1965.

Franke, Herbert. 'Could the Mongol Emperors read and write Chinese?' (*Asia Major,* new series, 3, 1, London, 1932) in Herbert Franke, *China Under Mongol Rule,* Aldershot, 1994.

'Europa in der Ostasiatischen Geschichtschreibung des 13 und 14 Jahrhunderts', *Saeculum,* 11, Freiburg in the Breslau, 1951.

'Sino-Western relations under the Mongol Empire' (*Journal of the Royal Asiatic Society Hong Kong Branch,* 6, Hong Kong, 1966) in Herbert Franke, *China Under Mongol Rule,* Aldershot, 1994.

'Some Sinological remarks on Rashid al-Din's History of China' (*Oriens,* 4/1, Leiden, 1951) in Herbert Franke, *China Under Mongol Rule,* Aldershot, 1994.

Freeman-Mitford, A. B. *The Attaché at Peking,* London, 1900.

Gallo, R. 'Marco Polo, la sua famiglia ed il suo libro', *Nel VII centario della nascità di Marco Polo,* Venice, 1955.

Gernet, Jacques. *Daily Life in China on the Eve of the Mongol Conquest,* Stanford, 1970.

Gil, Juan. *El libro de Marco Polo anotado por Cristobal Colon*, Madrid, 1987.

Gittings, John. *A Chinese view of China*, London, 1973.

Goodall, John. *Heaven and Earth: 120 album leaves from a Ming encyclopaedia*, London, 1979.

Grand Larousse Encyclopédique, Paris, 1964.

Haeger, John. 'Marco Polo in China? Problems with internal evidence', *Bulletin of Sung-Yuan Studies*, 14, New York, 1979.

Heers, Jacques. *Marco Polo*, Paris, 1982.

Hopkirk, Peter. *Foreign Devils on the Silk Road*, London, 1980.

Hughes, Robert. *Barcelona*, London, 1992.

D'Israeli, Isaac. *Amenities of Literature*, London, 1842.

Iwamura, Shinobu. *Manuscripts and Printed Editions of Marco Polo's Travels*, Tokyo, 1949.

Jackson, Peter. *The Mission of William of Rubruck*, London, 1990.

Jim Buhong. *In the Footsteps of Marco Polo*, Peking, 1989.

Jones, Mark (ed.). *Fake? The Art of Deception*, London, 1990.

Keay, J. *The Honourable Company*, London, 1993.

Kerr, Rose and Penelope Hughes-Stanton. *Kiln Sites of Ancient China*, London, 1980.

Kong, Demao. *The Mansion of Confucius*, London, 1989.

Lach, Donald. *Asia in the Making of Europe*, Chicago, 1965.

Latham, Ronald. *Marco Polo: The Travels*, Harmondsworth, 1958.

Lewis, Bernard. *The Muslim Discovery of Europe*, London, 1994.

Liddell, Caroline and Robin Weir. *Ices*, London, 1993.

Lieu, S. N. C. *Manichaeism in the Later Roman Empire and Medieval China*, Tubingen, 1992.

Lopez, R. S. 'China Silk in Europe in the Yuan period', *Journal of the American Oriental Society*, 72, New Haven, 1952.

Medley, Margaret. *The Chinese Potter*, Oxford, 1980.

Morgan, David. *The Mongols*, Oxford, 1986.

Moseley, C. W. R. D. (ed.). *The Travels of Sir John Mandeville*, Harmondsworth, 1983.

Moule, A. C. and Paul Pelliot. *Marco Polo: The Travels*, London, 1938.

Murray, Hugh. *The Travels of Marco Polo*, Edinburgh, 1847.

Needham, Joseph (ed.). *Science and Civilisation in China*, Cambridge, 1954.

Olschki, Leonardo. *Guillaume Boucher: a French artist at the court of the Khans*, Baltimore, 1946.
(ed.) *Il Milione*, Firenze, 1928.
Marco Polo's Asia, Berkeley, 1960.
'Une question d'onomatologie chinoise', *Oriens*, 3, Leiden, 1950.
Pelliot, Paul. *Notes on Marco Polo*, Paris, 1959–63.
Review of Charignon's re-edition of Pauthier's *Le Livre de Marco Polo*, in *T'oung Pao*, 25, Leiden, 1927.
Petech, L. 'Les marchands italiens dans l'empire Mongole', *Journal Asiatique*, Paris, 1962.
Phillips, J. R. S. *The Medieval Expansion of Europe*, Oxford, 1988.
Polo, Marco. *Il libro di Marco Polo detto Milione*, Turin, 1954.
Prestwich, Michael. *Edward I*, London, 1988.
Rachewiltz, Igor de. *Papal Envoys to the Great Khans*, London, 1971.
Reischauer, E. O. and J. K. Fairbank. *East Asia: the Great Tradition*, Boston, 1960.
Ricci, Aldo (trans.). *The Travels of Marco Polo*, London, 1931.
Roden, Claudia. *The Food of Italy*, London, 1989.
Ross, Sir Edward Denison. 'Marco Polo and his Book', London, 1935 (Annual Italian lecture of the British Academy, 1934).
Rossabi, M. *Khubilai Khan*, Berkeley, 1988.
Rouleau, F. 'The Yangchow Latin tombstone as a landmark of medieval Christianity in China', *Harvard Journal of Asiatic Studies*, 17, Cambridge, Mass., 1954.
Runiciman, Sir Stephen. *The Medieval Manichee*, Cambridge, 1947.
Sickman, L. and A. Soper. *The Art and Architecture of China*, Harmondsworth, 1971.
Silk and Rayon Users Association (ed.). *The Silk Book*, London, 1951.
Singer, Aburey. *The Lion and the Dragon*, London, 1992.
Southern, R. W. *The Making of the Middle Ages*, London, 1967.
Staunton, Sir George. *An authentic account of the embassy from the King of Great Britain to the Emperor of China*, Dublin, 1798.

Stein, Sir Mark Aurel. *Ruins of Desert Cathay*, (London, 1912)
New York, 1987.

Tsien Tsuen-hsuin. 'Paper and Printing', in Joseph Needham
(ed.), *Science and Civilisation in China*, vol 5, part 1,
Cambridge, 1985.

Twitchett, D. C. *Printing and Publishing in Medieval China*,
London, 1983.

Vainker, Shelagh. *Chinese Pottery and Porcelain*, London, 1991.

Vaughan, R. *The illustrated chronicles of Matthew Paris*, Stroud,
1993.

Vissière, I. and J.-L. (eds.). *Lettres édifiantes et curieuses de Chine
par des missionaires jésuites 1702–1776*, Paris, 1979.

Waldron, Arthur N. 'The problem of the Great Wall', *Harvard
Journal of Asiatic Studies*, 43/2, Cambridge, Mass., 1983.
The Great Wall of China, Cambridge, 1992.

Watson, W. (ed.). *The Genius of China*, London, 1973.

Wittkower, R. 'Marco Polo and the pictorial tradition of the
Marvels of the East' in R. Wittkower, *Allegory and the
Migration of Symbols*, London, 1977.

Yang Zhijiu. 'Make Poluo li hua de yi duan hanwen jicai' in
Xu Shixiong, *Make Poluo jieshao yu yanjiu*, Peking, 1983.

Yule, Colonel Sir Henry. *Cathay and the Way Thither*, London,
1916.
The Travels of Marco Polo: the complete Yule-Cordier edition,
(London, 1903, 1920), New York, 1993.

Index

Index